KITCHEN
TABLE

100 Essential Curries

KITCHEN TABLE gives you a wealth of recipes from your favourite chefs. Whether you want a quick weekday supper, sumptuous weekend feast or food for friends and family, let Rick, Ken, Madhur, Antonio, Ainsley, Mary and Annabel bring their expertise to your table.

For exclusive recipes, our regular newsletter, blog and news about Apps for your phone, visit www.mykitchentable.co.uk

Throughout this book, when you see **my** KITCHEN TABLE visit our site for practical videos, tips and hints from the My Kitchen Table team.

KITCHEN
TABLE

100 Essential Curries

MADHUR JAFFREY

www.mykitchentable.co.uk

Welcome to MY KITCHEN TABLE

The 100 recipes in this book include everything from a
Sweet and Sour Chicken Rizala, fit for a grand dinner, to
Hard-boiled Eggs Masala, a simple family supper.
If you like these recipes, you'll find more like them in the
rest of the series.

Contents

Pappadums or Papars

Pappadums or papars can be bought in delicatessens in two basic
varieties – spiced and unspiced. The spiced ones often have a liberal
sprinkling of crushed black pepper. They are deep-fried in hot oil and
served at cocktail parties. The frying takes just a few seconds. Papars
cannot be fried too far in advance, as any moisture in the air tends to
make them go limp and they should be crisp. Papars come in several
sizes. The large ones can be broken in half and then fried. They expand
a bit as they are cooked. Before you set out to make them, put a large
platter, well lined with kitchen paper, beside the stove to drain the papars.

Step One Heat the oil in a frying pan over medium heat. When
hot, put in one papar. It should sizzle and expand immediately.
(If it doesn't, your oil is not hot enough.) Turn it over, leave for
a few seconds, and remove with a slotted spoon. Place on a
prepared platter with paper towels, and drain.

Step Two Continue as above with all the remaining papars, one
at a time. If they begin to brown, your oil is too hot. Serve warm
or at room temperature with drinks.

Serves 8

8–10 papars or
pappadums

oil for deep-frying,
enough for 5cm (2in)
in a 25cm (10in) frying
pan

Onion Fritters

Even though these are served as a first course in many restaurants – and there is no reason why they should not be – in India they are generally served as a snack with tea. They may also be served with drinks. This particular recipe, in which an egg is used in the batter, comes from my friend, Badi Uzzaman, who played the part of my husband in the television series *Firm Friends*. A chutney should be served on the side.

Serves 6

1 large egg

1 tablespoon lemon juice

100g (4oz) chickpea flour (also called gram flour or besan)

¾ teaspoon salt

½ teaspoon chilli powder

½ teaspoon garam masala

½ teaspoon cumin seeds

1 teaspoon ground cumin

¼ teaspoon ground turmeric

1 fresh, hot green chilli, finely chopped

2 tablespoons chopped green coriander

vegetable oil for deep-frying

200g (7oz) onions, peeled and chopped into medium-sized dice

Step One Break the egg into a bowl and beat well. Add 4 tablespoons water and the lemon juice. Mix, add all the chickpea flour and mix well with a whisk. Put in the salt, chilli powder, garam masala, cumin seeds, ground cumin, turmeric, green chilli and green coriander. Mix well and set aside for at least 10 minutes or longer. Mix again with a whisk. The batter should be of a droppable consistency.

Step Two Put the oil for deep-frying in a wok or deep fryer and set over medium heat. You should have at least 7.5cm (3in) oil in the centre of the wok. When hot, put the onions into the batter and mix. (This should always be done just before frying.) Remove heaped teaspoons of the batter and drop it into the hot oil. Use up all the batter this way. Stir and fry the fritters for 7–8 minutes or until they are a golden red. Remove with a slotted spoon and drain on a plate lined with kitchen paper. Serve the fritters hot, as soon as they are made.

Sour Potatoes (Khatte Aloo)

This is an adaptation of a street-side snack to be found in different forms all over North India.

Step One Peel the cooled potatoes and dice them into 1cm (½in) cubes. Place in a large bowl. Add the remaining ingredients. Mix well. Check to see if salt and lemon juice are in correct proportions. To serve, place the potatoes on a platter accompanied by toothpicks. Serve with drinks.

Serves 10–12

7 medium-sized potatoes, boiled ahead of time, and set aside for at least 2 hours to cool

1½ teaspoons salt or to taste

2–3 tablespoons lemon juice or to taste

2 teaspoons ground roasted cumin

¼ teaspoon freshly ground black pepper

¼–½ teaspoon cayenne pepper

2 tablespoons finely chopped fresh green coriander

Spicy Vegetable Fritters (Pakoris)

Pakoris are similar to Japanese tempura. They are generally eaten with tea, but can also be served with drinks. I have specified potatoes in this recipe, but cauliflower florets, onion rings and peppers are equally good. A karhai is similar to a Chinese wok. It has a rounded base and is almost semi-circular in shape. It is particularly good for deep-frying as it allows you to use a relatively small amount of oil to obtain a good depth in the pan to submerge foods. The Plain Tamarind Chutney on page 199 is the perfect dip to serve with pakoris, though if you're feeling lazy you could serve Chinese duck sauce, tomato ketchup, or a combination of soy sauce, white vinegar and grated fresh ginger with a dash of Tabasco.

Serves 6–8

for the batter

100g (4oz) chickpea flour (besan)

1 teaspoon salt

¼ teaspoon ground turmeric

¼ teaspoon ground cumin

¼ teaspoon bicarbonate of soda

⅛ teaspoon freshly ground pepper

⅛ teaspoon cayenne pepper (optional)

for the filling

3 medium potatoes, peeled (or other vegetables, see above)

vegetable oil for deep-frying

salt and freshly ground black pepper

to serve

Plain Tamarind Chutney (see page 199)

Step One To make the batter, sift the chickpea flour into a bowl. Gradually mix in about 200ml (7fl oz) water until you have a fairly thick batter – thick enough to coat the vegetables. Add the other batter ingredients and mix well.

Step Two Cut the potatoes into thin rounds, 1mm ($\frac{1}{16}$in) thick, and immerse them in a bowl of cold water.

Step Three Pour sufficient oil into a wok, karhai or other deep-frying pan to give a 6–7.5cm (2½–3in) depth in the middle. Place over a low heat until hot, but not smoking. Take a few potato slices at a time, wipe them dry and dip them in the batter. Now drop them into the oil in a single layer. Fry slowly for 7–10 minutes on each side, until they are golden brown and cooked through. Remove with a slotted spoon and drain on kitchen paper. Sprinkle with salt and pepper and keep hot while cooking the rest of the *pakoris* in the same way. Serve the *pakoris* while they are crisp and hot, with the Plain Tamarind Chutney as a dip.

Prawns with Garlic and Chillies

Prawns cook so fast. The only time you will spend here is in peeling and de-veining them. I like to do this ahead of time and then keep them, washed and patted dry, in a polythene bag in the refrigerator, just ready to be stir-fried. They are perfect as a cocktail snack with toothpicks stuck in them, and also as a first course. You may serve them as a main dish as well. You will find that this recipe will serve six people as a first course or three to four people as a main one.

Step One Put the prawns in a bowl. Sprinkle the turmeric and chilli powder over them evenly and rub in.

Step Two Put the oil in a wok or large frying pan and set over a high heat. When very hot, put in the mustard seeds. As soon as they begin to pop – this takes just a few seconds – add the garlic. Stir until the garlic has turned golden. Add the green chilli. Stir once or twice. Add the prawns; stir and fry them over high heat until they just turn opaque. This will take 2–3 minutes. Sprinkle with salt and toss. Finally, sprinkle with the green coriander, then toss and serve.

Serves 6–8

450g (1lb) medium-sized, raw, headless prawns, peeled, de-veined and washed, then patted dry

¼ teaspoon ground turmeric

¼ teaspoon chilli powder

4 tablespoons vegetable oil

½ teaspoon black or yellow mustard seeds

5 garlic cloves, peeled and finely chopped

1 fresh, hot green chilli, finely chopped

½ teaspoon salt

2 teaspoons finely chopped green coriander or parsley

Delicious Chicken Bits

These wonderful chicken cubes may be served hot, warm or cold. They may be pierced with toothpicks and nibbled upon with drinks, added to salads or eaten at picnics. (The chicken bits may also be eaten as a main course with rice or potatoes and a green salad, when this recipe will serve four.) You may be surprised by my use of thyme. It tastes somewhat like our ajwain seeds, which are much harder to find. If you can get these, use about one third of a teaspoon only, as they are quite strong in flavour.

Serves 6–8

550g (1¼ lb) boned, skinned chicken breasts (4 breast pieces)

1 teaspoon freshly ground black pepper

¼ teaspoon ground turmeric

¼ teaspoon chilli powder

1 teaspoon ground cumin

1 teaspoon dried thyme

¼ teaspoon garlic powder

1 teaspoon bright red paprika

¼ teaspoon salt

vegetable oil

Step One Preheat the oven to 180°C/350°F/gas mark 4. Cut each chicken breast piece into thirds, lengthways, and then crossways into 2–2½cm (¾–1in) segments. Put in a bowl. Add the black pepper, turmeric, chilli powder, cumin, thyme, garlic powder, paprika, salt and 1 tablespoon of oil. Mix well and set aside for 10 minutes or longer.

Step Two Heat 2 tablespoons of oil in a wok or large, non-stick frying pan over very high heat. When very hot, put in the chicken. Stir and fry quickly until the chicken pieces are lightly browned or turn opaque on the outside. Put in a baking dish, cover loosely with lightly oiled greaseproof paper which should sit inside the dish and directly on the chicken pieces, and bake for about 8–10 minutes or until the chicken pieces are just cooked through. If not eating immediately, remove the chicken pieces from the hot baking dish to prevent them from drying out.

Chicken Livers with Fennel and Black Pepper (Murgh Ki Masedar Kaleji)

Cook these livers lightly, so there is just a hint of pink inside them. You may serve them as a first course or on toast as a snack.

Step One Put the turmeric, cumin, coriander, chilli powder and mustard into a small bowl along with 2 tablespoons water. Mix together well and set this spice paste aside.

Step Two Put the oil in a wok or a frying pan and set over high heat. When hot, put in the fennel seeds, curry leaves and garlic. Stir and fry until the garlic turns golden. Add the chicken livers. Sprinkle with ½ teaspoon salt and lots of black pepper. Stir and toss for 3–4 minutes or until nicely browned.

Step Three Remove the livers with a slotted spoon and put in a serving dish or bowl. Add the spice paste. Stir for 15 seconds or so. Add the cream and a light sprinkling of salt. Stir for 30–60 seconds or until the cream is slightly reduced. Pour the sauce over the chicken livers, sprinkle the green coriander over the top and serve.

Serves 4–8

¼ teaspoon ground turmeric

1 teaspoon ground cumin

1 teaspoon ground coriander

¼ teaspoon chilli powder

1 tablespoon grainy French mustard

3 tablespoons vegetable oil

¼ teaspoon fennel or anise seeds

10 fresh curry leaves, if available

3 garlic cloves, peeled and finely chopped

450g (1lb) chicken livers, trimmed and separated into 2 lobes each

salt and freshly ground black pepper

8 tablespoons single cream

3 tablespoons finely chopped green coriander

Gingery Cauliflower Soup

This soup may be served as an elegant first course at a grand dinner or as part of a simple lunch accompanied, perhaps, by a sandwich or salad or both. It may be made a day in advance and refrigerated. Reheat gently. It is a good idea to have the cumin, coriander, turmeric and chilli powder all measured into a small bowl before you start, as they go in together and cook very briefly.

Serves 4–6

3 tablespoons vegetable oil

175g (6oz) onions, peeled and chopped

2.5cm (1in) piece fresh ginger, peeled and cut into fine slivers

4 garlic cloves, peeled and chopped

1 teaspoon ground cumin

2 teaspoons ground coriander

¼ teaspoon ground turmeric

⅛–¼ teaspoon chilli powder

225g (8oz) potatoes, peeled and cut into rough 1cm (½ in) dice

225g (8oz) cauliflower florets

1.2 litres (2 pints) chicken stock

salt, if needed

150ml (5fl oz) single cream

Step One Set the oil over highish heat in a good-sized saucepan. When hot, add the onions, ginger and garlic. Stir and fry for about 4 minutes or until the onions are somewhat browned. Put in the cumin, coriander, turmeric and chilli powder. Stir once and add the potatoes, cauliflower and chicken stock. If the stock is unsalted, add ¼ teaspoon salt. Stir and bring to a boil. Cover, turn the heat to low and simmer gently for 10 minutes or until the potatoes are tender.

Step Two Taste for salt, adding more if you like. Put the soup into a blender, in 2 batches or more as required, and blend thoroughly. Strain, pushing down to get all the pulp. Add the cream and mix. The soup may now be reheated and served.

Madras Curry Soup

The origins of this recipe lie in an old Anglo-Indian cookery book. It is very much a 'Raj' period soup, and has the old-fashioned taste of hotel soups that I associate with my holidays in distant Himalayan resorts as a child in British India. Serve hot or cold, with thin, crisp toast.

Serves 4–6

Step One Put the oil in a pan and set over medium–high heat. When hot, add the onion. Sauté for 4–5 minutes or until the onion is golden. Add the curry powder and stir for 10 seconds. Now add the tomatoes, carrots, potatoes, peas, salt and 1 litre (1¾ pints) water. Bring to the boil. Cover, turn the heat to low and simmer gently for 45 minutes.

Step Two Blend the soup in batches in a blender, then strain it through a coarse sieve. Make sure you collect all the pulp under the sieve. Return the soup to the pan. Add the cream and stir. Now add the stock, adjusting the amount according to the thickness of soup you want. Stir to mix well. Reheat the soup, if you want it hot, or cover and refrigerate if you want it cold. Garnish with the chopped chives to serve.

2 tablespoons vegetable oil

1 medium onion, peeled and chopped

2 tablespoons curry powder

450g (1lb) coarsely chopped tomatoes

2 medium carrots, peeled and cut into rounds

350g (12oz) potatoes, peeled and cut into rough dice

120g (4½ oz) peas, fresh, or frozen and defrosted

2¼ teaspoons salt, or to taste

250ml (8floz) double cream

approximately 250ml (8fl oz) vegetable stock

1 tablespoon finely chopped fresh chives, to garnish (optional)

Glorious Seafood Soup

You can improvise freely here and add seafood that you happen to like. I often put in squid, cut into rings, and cubes of filleted white fish, such as sole. When you are selecting shellfish, avoid mussels or clams that have broken or damaged shells.

Serves 4

16 mussels

8 clams

100g (4oz) raw, headless prawns

1cm (½ in) cube fresh root ginger

40g (1½ oz) onion

1.2 litres (2 pints) chicken stock

1 teaspoon black peppercorns

salt

40g (1½ oz) unsalted butter

3 tablespoons plain flour

50g (2oz) cooked or uncooked white crab meat

5 tablespoons thick coconut milk

chopped fresh parsley, to garnish

Step One Rinse the mussels and clams thoroughly under cold running water to help rid them of sand and grit. Scrub them well with a stiff brush under cold running water. Pull off and discard the 'beards' from the mussels. Tap any open molluscs with the back of a knife. If they refuse to close, discard them. Wash the molluscs again; set aside. Peel and de-vein the prawns, rinse, then pat dry. Cut each prawn crossways into 3 segments; set aside.

Step Two Cut the ginger crossways into 4–5 slices. Peel the onion. Combine the stock, ginger, whole onion and peppercorns in a pan and bring to a simmer. Cover and simmer gently for 15 minutes. Strain the stock into a clean pan. Add a little salt – allowing for the saltiness of the shellfish; keep hot.

Step Three Melt the butter in a wide, heavy pan. Add the flour and cook, stirring, over a low heat for 2 minutes, until bubbling but not brown. Slowly pour in the hot stock, stirring rapidly with a whisk. Simmer gently for 3–4 minutes. (If any lumps appear, strain at this stage.)

Step Four Add the mussels and clams to the soup and bring to the boil. Cover, turn the heat to medium and cook for 5 minutes, or until the shells have opened up. (If some have not, cook for another minute, then discard any that remain closed.) Put in the prawns, crab meat and coconut milk. Cook over a low heat for 1 minute. Serve the soup in wide soup plates, garnished with chopped parsley.

Prawns in a Tomato–Cream Sauce

One of the aromas that I find very refreshing in this dish is that of fresh curry leaves. Sadly they are not always easy to find. If you can get only dried leaves, mix them into the sauce instead of frying them with the prawns. If you cannot find any, the dish will still taste superb without.

Step One To make the sauce, put the tomato purée in a bowl and add the salt, sugar, garam masala, ground roasted cumin seeds, chilli powder, green coriander, green chilli, lemon juice and 1 tablespoon water. Mix well. Slowly add the coconut milk or cream, mixing as you go. Set aside.

Step Two To stir-fry the prawns, peel and finely chop the garlic, then put 3 tablespoons oil in a wok or frying pan and set over highish heat. When hot, add the mustard seeds. As soon as the mustard seeds begin to pop – this takes just a few seconds – put in the garlic and curry leaves. Stir until the garlic turns medium brown and add the prawns. Stir until the prawns turn opaque most of the way through and add the sauce. Turn the heat to medium and just heat the sauce through until it begins to simmer. By then the prawns should be completely opaque and cooked through. Remove from the heat and serve.

Serves 4-5

for the sauce

1 tablespoon tomato purée

¼ teaspoon salt

¼ teaspoon sugar

1 teaspoon garam masala

½ teaspoon ground roasted cumin seeds

⅛–¼ teaspoon chilli powder or to taste

3 tablespoons finely chopped coriander

1 fresh hot green chilli, finely chopped

1 tablespoon lemon juice

200ml (7fl oz) tinned coconut milk, stirred, or single cream

for the prawns

vegetable oil

1 teaspoon black mustard seeds

3 garlic cloves

10–15 curry leaves

550 g (1¼ lb) medium-sized, raw, headless prawns, peeled, de-veined and washed

Spicy Prawn and Cucumber Curry

This curry is actually made with bottle gourd – a pale green vegetable, shaped like a bowling pin. You can easily use cucumber instead as its taste is similar when cooked. The origins of this Malay dish probably lie in India – the use of ground coriander and fennel seeds, as well as the final popping of seasonings in hot oil, all testify to that.

Serves 4–6

275g (10oz) cucumber

100g (4oz) shallots or onions

6 garlic cloves

2 tablespoons ground coriander seeds

1 tablespoon ground fennel seeds (see Tip below)

½–1 teaspoon ground white pepper, or to taste

1 tablespoon ground cumin seeds

1 teaspoon ground turmeric

3–4 dried hot red chillies

350g (12oz) raw, headless prawns, peeled, de-veined and washed

¾–1 teaspoon salt

1 teaspoon sugar

400 ml (14fl oz) thick coconut milk

4 tablespoons vegetable oil

1 teaspoon whole fennel seeds

Step One Peel the cucumber and cut crossways into 1cm (½in) thick rounds. Peel the shallots and finely chop three quarters of them; finely slice the rest. Peel the garlic cloves. Chop four of them *very* finely; cut the other two into fine slivers. Combine the sliced shallots and slivered garlic and set these aside.

Step Two In a medium pan, combine the chopped shallots, chopped garlic, ground coriander seeds, ground fennel seeds, white pepper, cumin seeds, turmeric and 450ml (15fl oz) water. Crumble in the red chillies. Stir and bring to the boil. Boil, uncovered, on a fairly high heat for about 5 minutes.

Step Three Add the cucumber rounds and bring to a simmer. Cover and simmer gently for 5 minutes. Add the prawns, salt and sugar. Bring to a simmer again and simmer gently for about 1 minute, stirring the prawns around in the sauce. Give the coconut milk a good stir and pour it in. Bring the mixture to the boil, then lower the heat and simmer for 1 minute, stirring now and then.

Step Four Put the oil in a small frying pan and set over a medium–high heat. When hot, add the slivered shallots and garlic and stir-fry until they turn golden. Add the whole fennel seeds, stir once, then quickly pour the contents of the pan (oil and seasonings) into the pan containing the curry. Cover the curry pan immediately to trap all the aromas. Serve with rice.

Tip

If you cannot get ground fennel seeds, simply grind whole seeds in a clean coffee grinder.

Prawns with Crushed Mustard Seeds

This recipe originates from Bengal, where a paste made from ground black mustard seeds is often added to fish to give it a very special nose-tingling pungency. Serve with a rice dish, one or two vegetable side dishes and a natural yoghurt relish.

Step One Crush the mustard seeds, using a pestle and mortar or spice or coffee grinder.

Step Two In a small bowl, mix the crushed mustard seeds, turmeric and tomato purée, together with 3 tablespoons hot water. Set aside.

Step Three Heat the oil in a large frying pan over a medium–high heat. Add the garlic cloves, ginger slices and dried chilli and fry, stirring, for a few seconds until the mixture begins to darken, then add the prawns. Fry, stirring, until the prawns turn opaque. Stir in the mustard seed paste and turn the heat to medium–low. Add the salt, pepper and lemon or lime juice. Fry, stirring, for a further 2 minutes. Transfer to a warm serving dish.

Serves 3–4

1 teaspoon black mustard seeds

⅛ teaspoon ground turmeric

2 teaspoons tomato purée

4 tablespoons mustard oil, or other vegetable oil

2 garlic cloves, peeled

2 thin slices fresh root ginger, peeled

1 hot dried red chilli

450g (1lb) raw, headless prawns, peeled, de-veined and washed

¼ teaspoon salt

large pinch of freshly ground black pepper

1 tablespoon lemon or lime juice

Have you made this recipe? Tell us what you think at
www.mykitchentable.co.uk/blog

Prawn Pullao

This pullao can be cooked with prawns or with any firm-fleshed fish like cod or halibut. Serve with Green Beans with Fresh Coconut and Sesame Seeds and any natural yoghurt side dish.

Serves 6

350g (12oz) raw, headless prawns, peeled, de-veined and washed

3 tablespoons finely chopped fresh green coriander

1 teaspoon ground turmeric

1 teaspoon garam masala

1½ teaspoon salt

1 tablespoon lemon juice

½–1 fresh hot green chilli, finely sliced (optional)

4 tablespoons vegetable oil

1 medium-sized onion

350g (12oz) long-grain rice

Step One After rinsing the prawns, pat them dry with kitchen paper.

Step Two In a teacup, mix 1 tablespoon warm water, the chopped green coriander, turmeric, garam masala, ½ teaspoon salt, the lemon juice and green chilli.

Step Three Heat 2 tablespoons oil in a 25cm (10in) frying pan over medium–low heat. Pour in the contents of the cup and fry, stirring, for 2 to 3 minutes. Add the prawns, and on a medium flame fry them with the spices for about 4 minutes. With a slotted spoon, remove the prawns to a covered dish, leaving the sauce behind.

Step Four Pour 275ml (9fl oz) warm water into the frying pan and scrape up all the spices stuck to the bottom and sides, turning up the heat if necessary. Peel the onion, cut into fine rounds and cut rounds in half.

Step Five In a heavy-bottomed 3½–5 litre (6–8 pint) pot, heat the remaining oil over medium heat. Put in the sliced onions, and fry them for 3–4 minutes until the edges begin to turn brown. Now add the rice, 450ml (15fl oz) water, 1 teaspoon salt and the liquid from the frying pan. Stir and bring to the boil, then cover and reduce heat to very low. Cook for 25 minutes.

Step Six Lift the cover off the saucepan and add the prawns. Mix quickly with a fork and cover again. Cook another 5 minutes.

Prawns, Crab or Lobster, Kerala Style

This dish comes from Kerala, a state along India's south-western coast. Roasted coconut is added to the seafood to give it a thick sauce. It is quite delicious. Serve with a rice dish and a dal (see pages 157–171).

Step One Heat oil either in a deep 25cm (10in) frying pan or in a 25cm (10in) heavy-bottomed pot over a medium–high flame. Add the chopped onions and fry, stirring, for 7–8 minutes or until the onions are slightly browned, but soft. Turn off the heat.

Step Two In a blender container, combine the ginger, garlic, tomatoes and grated roasted coconut. Blend at high speed until you have a paste. Add the contents of the blender container to the frying pan or pot. Also add the turmeric, coriander, cayenne, tamarind paste, salt and 150ml (5fl oz) water. Bring to the boil. Cover, lower heat, and simmer gently for 5 minutes. (This much of the recipe can be made up to a day in advance. Keep covered and refrigerated until ready for use.)

Step Three Seven to 8 minutes before serving, bring the sauce to the boil. Add the prawns or lobster meat or crabmeat, fold in, and cook at high temperature, stirring continuously, until the meat turns opaque (about 5 minutes). The sauce should be very thick and cling to the meat, but if you desire a thinner sauce add a bit more water.

Serves 4–6

3 tablespoons vegetable oil

2 medium-sized onions, peeled and finely chopped

0.5cm (¼ in) piece fresh ginger, peeled

4 garlic cloves, peeled and chopped

3 medium-sized tomatoes (tinned or fresh), peeled and chopped

½ teacup grated and roasted fresh coconut

½ teaspoon ground turmeric

1 tablespoon ground coriander, roasted

¼ teaspoon cayenne pepper

3 tablespoons tamarind paste

½–¾ teaspoon salt

900g (2lb) medium-sized, raw, headless prawns, peeled, de-veined and washed, or 900g (2lb) uncooked lobster meat, cut into 2.5cm (1in) pieces, or 900g (2lb) uncooked crabmeat, cut into bite-sized sections

Scallops in a Spinach–Tomato Curry Sauce

This dish may be eaten with rice or, oddly enough, with noodles. It is superb for entertaining. You could, if you like, make it with prawns.

Serves 4

½ teaspoon chilli powder

½ teaspoon ground turmeric

1 teaspoon ground cumin

1 teaspon ground coriander

1½ teaspoons salt

freshly ground black pepper

1 teaspoon grainy French mustard

vegetable oil

1 teaspoon black or yellow mustard seeds

3–4 garlic cloves, peeled and finely chopped

1cm (½ in) piece fresh ginger, peeled and finely chopped

150ml (5fl oz) tinned chopped tomatoes

100g (4 oz) fresh spinach, cut crossways into fine strips

550g (1¼ lb) whole raw scallops

120ml (4fl oz) tinned coconut milk, stirred, or single cream

Step One Combine the chilli powder, turmeric, cumin, coriander, salt, black pepper, French mustard and 2 tablespoons water in a small bowl. Mix.

Step Two Put 3 tablespoons oil in a large, non-stick frying pan and set over high heat. When hot, put in the whole mustard seeds. As soon as they begin to pop – a matter of seconds – put in the garlic and ginger. Stir and fry until the garlic turns a light brown. Add the spice paste. Stir and fry for 15 seconds. Put in the tomatoes and spinach. Stir and cook for a minute. Add 250ml (8fl oz) water and bring to a simmer. Simmer, uncovered, on low heat for 10 minutes. Add the scallops. Turn the heat to high. Stir and cook until the scallops just turn opaque. This will happen quite fast. Add the coconut milk or cream and bring to a simmer. Stir and simmer for half a minute. Remove from the heat and serve.

Fish Fillets in a 'Curry' Sauce

Bland white sauces were anathema to the Indian cooks who presided over Anglo-Indian households, so they invariably added a few local seasonings in order to perk them up. Here is one such dish. You may use any fish fillets – cod, haddock and halibut – although fillets of dark, oily fish, such as blue fish and mackerel, are ideal. Get thick fillets if possible, and if the skin can be removed, so much the better.

Step One Arrange a shelf in the upper third of the oven and preheat the oven to its highest temperature. Spread the fish out in a somewhat deep dish. Combine the milk, salt, pepper, chilli powder and turmeric in a jug and pour over the fish. Set aside for 15 minutes. (Use this time to get all the remaining ingredients weighed, measured and chopped.) After the time is up, lift the fish out of the milk and dust both sides with the breadcrumbs, patting them on so that they adhere. Reserve the milk and put the fish in a shallow baking tray lined with foil. Dot with 25g (1oz) of the butter and bake for 15 minutes.

Step Two While the fish bakes, set the milk to heat. Melt the remaining butter in a small, heavy saucepan over medium–low heat. When it has melted and is bubbling, add the curry powder. Stir for a minute. Now add the flour. Stir for about 2 minutes. It should keep bubbling. Take the saucepan off the heat and, using a whisk, beat in the hot milk. Now put the saucepan on medium–high heat and stir with the whisk until the sauce comes to a boil. Boil for a minute, whisking all the time. Add the green coriander and lemon juice. Stir to mix them in. Put the fish on a serving plate or on individual plates. Pour the sauce over the top and serve immediately. Extra sauce, if there is any, may be served on the side.

Serves 4–5

900g (2lb) thick fish fillet or fillets

500ml (18fl oz) milk

1 teaspoon salt

lots of freshly ground black pepper

½ teaspoon chilli powder

¼ teaspoon ground turmeric

5 tablespoons breadcrumbs (made from dried bread – home-made or store-bought)

50g (2oz) unsalted butter

4 tablespoons good curry powder

2 tablespoons plain flour

3 tablespoons finely chopped green coriander

2–3 teaspoons lemon juice

Fried Fish Steaks

Halibut steaks with bone are ideal for this very satisfying dish, although other fish steaks such as salmon or mackerel may be used. It may be served as part of an Indian meal or Western-style with boiled potatoes and a salad or cooked vegetable.

Serves 3

3 medium-sized halibut steaks (about 630g/1lb 6oz)

⅓–½ teaspoon salt

⅓–½ teaspoon freshly ground black pepper

¼ teaspoon ground turmeric

¼ teaspoon chilli powder, or to taste

½ teaspoon store-bought garam masala

1 tablespoon plain flour

4 tablespoons vegetable oil

3 lemon wedges

Step One Lay the fish pieces out in a single layer on a big plate. Dust evenly on both sides with the salt, black pepper, turmeric, chilli powder and garam masala. Rub the spices in. Now dust both sides with the flour and let the steaks sit for 10–15 minutes.

Step Two Put the oil in a large frying pan and set over medium–high heat. When hot, put in the steaks in a single layer. When one side turns golden-brown, turn the fish pieces over carefully and brown the second side as well. The fish is done when it is just cooked through. Remove with a slotted spatula and serve with the lemon wedges.

For more recipes from My Kitchen Table, sign up for our newsletter at www.mykitchentable.co.uk/newsletter

Afsha Mumtaz's Dry Masala Fish (Sookhi Macchi)

This is perhaps the most-loved fish dish in our family. What is more, it is very easy to prepare.

Step One Wash the fish well, then pat dry with kitchen paper. Using a sharp knife, make deep, slightly diagonal slits across the fish on both sides at 2½cm (1in) intervals. Rub with ½ teaspoon salt, going well into the slits, stomach and cavities. Set aside for 10 minutes.

Step Two Combine the natural yoghurt, lemon juice, garam masala, cayenne pepper, ginger, garlic and ¼ teaspoon salt in a bowl and mix well. Rub most of this paste all over the fish, again going into all the slits on both sides and into the cavities. Retain about 2 tablespoons.

Step Three Place the fish on a rack set on a baking sheet (to catch the drippings) and set aside for 10 minutes. Meanwhile, preheat the grill, arranging a shelf so that the top of the fish will be a distance of about 13–15cm (5–6in) from the source of heat.

Step Four Drizzle half the oil over the top of the fish and grill for 9–10 minutes or until browned. Turn the sheet around halfway through this period to ensure even colouring. Now carefully turn over the fish. Spread the remaining spice paste on the second side (it will have lost some of its original marinade) and drizzle the remaining oil over the top. Grill this side for about 8 minutes or until it, too, is browned. Turn off the grill and heat the oven to 180°C/350°F/gas 4. Let the fish bake for 10 minutes. Serve immediately.

Serves 4

900g (2lb) red snapper

salt

6 tablespoons natural yoghurt

1 tablespoon lemon juice

2 teaspoons garam masala

1 teaspoon cayenne pepper

1 tablespoon peeled and finely grated fresh ginger

5 garlic cloves, peeled and crushed to a pulp

2 tablespoons corn oil, peanut oil or olive oil

Fish in a Green Sauce

You need a firm-fleshed fish here; king fish and salmon are ideal.

Serves 2

for the fish

2 good-sized salmon or king fish steaks (about 675g/1½ lb)

salt and freshly ground black pepper

⅛ teaspoon ground turmeric

⅛ teaspoon chilli powder

for the green sauce

vegetable oil

85g (3oz) onions, peeled and finely chopped

2 garlic cloves, peeled and finely chopped

1-teacup finely chopped coriander

1 medium tomato, finely chopped

2–3 fresh hot green chillies

1 teaspoon peeled, finely grated fresh ginger

1 tablespoon lemon juice

⅛ teaspoon salt

⅛ teaspoon chilli powder

½ teaspoon garam masala

Step One Rub the fish on both sides with a generous sprinkling of salt, lots of freshly ground pepper and the turmeric and chilli powder. Rub well and set aside.

Step Two Put 3 tablespoons oil in a non-stick frying pan and set over high heat. When hot, put in the fish and brown quickly on both sides without letting it cook through. Remove with a slotted spoon and set aside. Add the onion and garlic to the pan. Stir and fry until the onion browns a bit. Add the green coriander, tomato, green chillies, ginger, lemon juice and salt. Stir and cook over medium–high heat until the coriander and tomato have completely wilted. Spread the green sauce around in the frying pan and check the salt.

Step Three Lay the fish over the top. Now spoon some green sauce over the fish. Sprinkle the chilli powder and garam masala over the top. Bring to a simmer. Cover, lower the heat and simmer gently for about 10 minutes.

Spicy Grilled Fish

Fish is grilled all along India's coastline, using a variety of marinades and basting sauces. Sometimes the grilling is done over rice straw, at other times over smouldering coconut husks. I have used my indoor grill here but you could also grill outdoors over charcoal. What helps the grilling enormously is a hinged, double-racked 'holder'. The fish is placed securely inside it. It can then be turned and basted with ease. If you cannot find one, just oil your grill rack well and lay your fish directly on it.

Step One Wash the fish well and pat dry. Cut 3–4 deep, diagonal slits across both sides of the fish. Rub with ½ teaspoon salt and 1 tablespoon of the lemon juice. Set aside as you make the marinade.

Step Two Combine the remaining lemon juice, ¼ teaspoon salt, onion, garlic, ginger, green chilli, turmeric, garam masala and chilli powder in the container of an electric blender and blend until smooth. Empty the paste into a shallow dish large enough to hold the fish. Add the coconut milk and mix. Now put the fish into the dish and rub with the marinade. Leave for 5–10 minutes.

Step Three Meanwhile, preheat your indoor griil and oil your grilling rack with a little vegetable oil. The rack should be placed about 15cm (6in) from the source of heat. Lift the fish out of the marinade and place it in (or on) the rack. Grill for about 25 minutes, turning every 5 minutes and basting frequently with the marinade; if you do not have a hinged rack, turn only once, midway through the cooking, using the flat side of a large chef's knife. If the fish is browning too fast, distance it some more from the source of heat. Do not baste towards the end to allow the fish to form a crust.

Serves 2–3

550g (1¼ lb) trout, salmon trout or salmon, scaled, cleaned and left whole

salt

3 tablespoons lemon juice

50g (2oz) onion, peeled and coarsely chopped

2 garlic cloves, peeled and coarsely chopped

2.5cm (1in) piece fresh ginger

1 fresh, hot green chilli, sliced

¼ teaspoon ground turmeric

1 teaspoon garam masala

¼ teaspoon chilli powder

175ml (6fl oz) tinned coconut milk, well stirred

vegetable oil

Curried Tuna (Tuna Ki Kari)

This recipe, which is as good as it is simple, comes from Chun Kern, my friend from the Himalayan hills who now lives in the United States. You may eat this in sandwiches, on toast, take it on picnics (I always do) or use it as a stuffing for 'turnover'-type patties made with store-bought puff pastry. It is excellent eaten plain with a variety of salads. Use a good-quality tinned tuna packed in oil. I do not drain it as the oil prevents the tuna from drying out. Also, a good curry powder provides a useful short cut.

Serves 2–3

1½ tablespoons vegetable oil

50g (2oz) onion, peeled and cut into very fine half-rings

1 garlic clove, peeled and very finely chopped

1 teaspoon curry powder

1 x 175g (6oz) tin good-quality tuna, packed in oil

½–1 fresh, hot green chilli, cut into very fine rounds

1cm (½in) piece fresh ginger, peeled and cut into very fine slices, then into very fine strips

2–3 tablespoons chopped green coriander

salt, to taste

freshly ground black pepper

Step One Put the oil in a non-stick frying pan and set over medium–high heat. When hot, add the onion and garlic. Stir and fry until the onion turns brown at the edges. Put in the curry powder, stir once or twice. Add the tuna. Stir it around and break up any big lumps. Turn the heat to low. Add the green chilli, ginger and green coriander. Stir to mix. Check for salt, adding it if needed. Add a generous amount of black pepper. Mix well and turn off the heat. Serve hot, at room temperature or cold.

Sea Bass in Green Chutney

Here is my version of a very popular dish in which a whole fish is smothered in green chutney and then cooked in banana leaves. When I haven't any banana leaves handy, I use foil, which seems to work perfectly well. Serve the fish with plain basmati rice. Tomato and Onion Relish (see page 204) is an ideal accompaniment.

Step One Wash the fish thoroughly inside and out under cold running water, Pat dry, inside and out. Preheat the oven to 200°C/400°F/gas mark 6.

Step Two Peel and coarsely chop the ginger and garlic. Place them in an electric blender with 3 tablespoons water and blend to a smooth paste.

Step Three Heat the oil in a frying pan over a medium–high heat, add the mustard seeds and stir for a few seconds until they begin to expand and pop. Add the red peppers, and stir them once. Pour in the paste from the blender, add the turmeric and fry, stirring, for about 2 minutes.

Step Four Pour the contents of the frying pan into the blender. Add the coriander, lemon juice and salt. Blend to a smooth paste, adding up to 2 tablespoons of water if necessary.

Step Five Line a large baking dish with a sheet of foil, big enough to enclose the fish. Lay the fish on the foil and cover with the coriander paste, inside and out. Fold the foil over the fish to enclose it completely, Bake in the oven for 30 minutes. Carefully unwrap the fish and lift on to a warm platter. Spoon any green chutney in the foil on to the fish to serve.

Serves 2

675–900 g (1½–2lb) whole sea bass, with head and tail, cleaned

2.5cm (1in) cube fresh root ginger

5 garlic cloves

2 tablespoons vegetable oil

½ teaspoon black mustard seeds

2 whole hot dried red peppers (optional)

½ teaspoon ground turmeric

1 teacup chopped fresh green coriander leaves

2 tablespoons lemon juice

¼ teaspoon salt

Scrambled Eggs, Indian Style

While some Indians eat their scrambled eggs with toast, others eat them with hot parathas, chapatis or pooris.

Serves 2–3

3 tablespoons butter

½ medium onion, finely chopped

1 small tomato, chopped

1 tablespoon chopped fresh green coriander

½–1 hot green chilli, finely sliced

4 medium or large eggs, well beaten

salt and pepper, to taste

Step One Melt the butter in a 25cm (10in) frying pan over medium heat. Add the onion and sauté for a minute or until they begin to turn translucent. Add the chopped tomato, green coriander and sliced green chilli. Stir and cook for 3–4 minutes or until the tomatoes soften a bit.

Step Two Pour in the beaten eggs. Sprinkle on salt and pepper lightly. Stir and move the eggs around with a fork. Indians like their scrambled eggs rather hard (cooked about 3 minutes), but you can stop whenever the desired consistency has been achieved.

For more recipes from My Kitchen Table, sign up for our newsletter at www.mykitchentable.co.uk/newsletter

Eggs with Fresh Green Herbs (Hare Masale Ka Omlate)

This may be served at breakfasts and brunches as soon as it comes out of the frying pan (I serve it with toast) and may also be sliced and put into sandwiches to perk up a picnic or an office lunch. It is really a kind of flat egg pancake seasoned with spring onions, green coriander, green chillies, ginger and garlic. It is a good idea to have everything cut and ready before you start as this dish cooks very quickly.

Step One Break the eggs into a bowl and beat well. Add a generous ¼ teaspoon salt and lots of freshly ground black pepper.

Step Two Put the oil in a large, non-stick frying pan and set over medium–high heat. When hot, add the spring onions. Stir and fry until the onions just start to brown at the edges. Add the garlic and stir for a few seconds. Now put in the green coriander, chillies, ginger and turmeric. Stir for a few seconds. Add the lemon juice and sugar and stir to mix. Working quickly, spread the herbs around evenly in the pan.

Step Three Now pour in the beaten eggs and let them spread to the edges of the pan. Cover, turn the heat to medium–low and cook for a few minutes, just until the eggs have set. Cut into wedges and serve immediately.

Serves 2–4

5 large eggs

salt and freshly ground black pepper

2 tablespoons vegetable oil

3 spring onions, cut into fine rounds (the white as well as the green sections)

¼ teaspoon peeled, very finely chopped garlic

3 tablespoons finely chopped green coriander

1–2 fresh, hot green chillies, sliced into fine rounds

½ teaspoon peeled, very finely chopped fresh ginger

generous pinch of ground turmeric

1½ teaspoons lemon juice

⅓ teaspoon sugar

Hard-boiled Eggs 'Masala'

These can be whipped up quickly for lunch or supper. They may be served with rice or even bread (toasted or plain).

Serves 2–4

½ teaspoon chilli powder

½ teaspoon ground turmeric

1 teaspoon ground cumin

1 teaspoon ground coriander

1 teaspoon lemon juice

¼ teaspoon salt

freshly ground black pepper

2 tablespoons vegetable oil

½ teaspoon cumin seeds

75g (3oz) onion, peeled and finely chopped

1cm (½in) piece fresh ginger, peeled and finely chopped

250ml (8fl oz) tinned chopped tomatoes (or lightly drained, tinned whole tomatoes, finely chopped)

¼ teaspoon sugar

3–4 tablespoons chopped green coriander

4 hard-boiled eggs, peeled and cut into halves lengthways

Step One Combine the chilli powder, turmeric, ground cumin, ground coriander, lemon juice, salt, black pepper and 1 tablespoon water in a small bowl and mix.

Step Two Put the oil in a medium-sized, non-stick frying pan and set over highish heat. When hot, add the cumin seeds. Ten seconds later, add the onion and ginger. Stir and fry until the onion turns medium brown. Add the spice paste. Stir and cook for 15 seconds. Now add the tomatoes and sugar and bring to a simmer. Cover and simmer gently for 10 minutes.

Step Three Add the green coriander, stirring once or twice, then lay the cut eggs in the sauce and spoon more sauce over them. Cover and simmer gently for 2–3 minutes.

Spicy Grilled Chicken

Sometimes, after a long day at work, the easiest dish to put on the table is grilled chicken. Most Indian versions require a marinating period, but if you are rushed, as I am most of the time, follow this recipe and you will come up with delicious results – fast. The spice paste may be prepared up to a day ahead of time and refrigerated. You can also rub the chicken pieces with the spice paste and leave them for up to 24 hours before grilling. This chicken may be served, Western-style, with boiled potatoes and a green vegetable or salad. You may also serve it with rice and an Indian vegetable.

Step One Preheat the grill and arrange the grilling tray at least 13–15cm (5–6in) from the source of heat. If you can control your heat, set it at medium–high. Combine all the ingredients for the spice paste in a bowl and mix well. Rub the paste over the chicken as evenly as possible.

Step Two Arrange the chicken pieces on the grilling tray in a single layer, with the fleshier parts up and the skin side down. Grill for 10–12 minutes or until browned. You may need to rearrange some of the pieces, so that they all brown evenly. Turn the pieces over and cook the second side in the same way.

Serves 4

1 tablespoon coarsely crushed black peppercorns

1 tablespoon paprika (bright red, if possible)

½ teaspoon chilli powder, or to taste

1 tablespoon garam masala

2 teaspoons ground cumin

2 teaspoons oregano

1 garlic clove, peeled and crushed

1¼ teaspoons salt

3 tablespoons vegetable oil

2 tablespoons lemon juice

2 tablespoons natural yoghurt

1kg (2¼ lb) jointed chicken pieces

For a video masterclass on how to tell if your chicken is cooked, go to www.mykitchentable.co.uk /videos/cookingchicken

Quick Chicken Korma (Murgh Korma)

When trying to cook fast, it helps to have all the right utensils to hand. Here, a blender to make the ginger–garlic paste and a frying pan that holds all the chicken in a single layer will be of great help. This dish can be made a day ahead of time and refrigerated. It reheats well.

Serves 4

4cm (1½ in) piece fresh ginger, peeled and coarsely chopped

5–6 garlic cloves, peeled and coarsely chopped

6 tablespoons vegetable oil

3 bay leaves

5cm (2in) cinnamon stick

8 cardamom pods

4 cloves

¼ teaspoon black cumin seeds

120g (4½ oz) onions, peeled and finely chopped

1 tablespoon ground coriander

1 tablespoon ground cumin

3 tinned plum tomatoes, chopped

1.5kg (3lb) chicken pieces, skinned and cut into serving portions

¼ –1 teaspoon chilli powder

¼ teaspoon salt

3 tablespoons single cream

Step One Put the ginger, garlic and 3 tablespoons water in the container of an electric blender. Blend until you have a smooth paste.

Step Two Put the oil in a wide frying pan or sauté pan and set over high heat. When very hot, put in the bay leaves, cinnamon, cardamom pods, cloves and cumin seeds. Stir once or twice and add the onions. Stir and fry for about 3 minutes or until the onions turn brownish. Add the paste from the blender, and the ground coriander and ground cumin, and fry for a minute. Add the chopped tomatoes and fry for another minute. Add the chicken pieces, chilli powder, salt and 250ml (8fl oz) water. Bring to a boil. Cover, turn the heat to medium and cook for 15 minutes, turning the chicken pieces over now and then.

Step Three Remove the cover, add the cream and cook on high heat for another 7–8 minutes or until the sauce has thickened. Stir gently as you do this.

Minced Chicken with Peas

Minced chicken – or turkey, for that matter – cooks in minutes. If a guest unexpectedly shows up, this may be the perfect dish to serve. I have used peas here, but infinite variations are possible: cooked broad beans, cut up and cooked green beans, even corn kernels, may be added to the mince.

Step One Put the oil in a wide pan and set over medium–high heat. When hot, add the cinnamon stick, cardamom pods and bay leaves. Stir for a few seconds. Add the onions. Stir and fry until the onion pieces turn brown at the edges. Add the garlic and stir for a few seconds. Add the ginger and stir for another few seconds. Now add the chicken (or turkey). Stir and fry until all the lumps are broken up. Add all the remaining ingredients. Stir to mix and cook for another 2–3 minutes, stirring as you do so.

Note

The large spices are not meant to be eaten.

Serves 3–4

3 tablespoons vegetable oil

2.5cm (1in) cinnamon stick

4 cardamom pods

2 bay leaves

100g (4oz) onions, peeled and chopped

3 garlic cloves, peeled and finely chopped

2 teaspoons peeled, finely grated fresh ginger

550 g (1¼ lb) minced chicken (or turkey)

175–200g (6–7oz) lightly cooked fresh or frozen peas

¼ teaspoon ground turmeric

1 teaspoon store-bought garam masala

¼ teaspoon chilli powder

½–¾ teaspoon salt

2 tablespoons lemon juice

freshly ground black pepper

Easy Chicken Kebabs

You may serve these kebabs with drinks, as a first course or even as a light main dish. The pieces of meat may be skewered before grilling or they may just be spread out on a grilling tray.

Serves 4

4 boned, skinned chicken breast halves (about 550g/1¼ lb)

¾ teaspoon salt

2 tablespoons lemon juice

3 tablespoons natural yoghurt

1 tablespoon chickpea flour (also called gram flour or besan)

1 teaspoon peeled, very finely grated fresh ginger

2 garlic cloves, peeled and crushed to a pulp

¼ teaspoon chilli powder

¼ teaspoon ground turmeric

½ teaspoon ground cumin

½ teaspoon garam masala

4 tablespoons melted butter or vegetable oil for basting

Step One Cut each breast half into halves, lengthways, and cut crossways into 2.5cm (1in) pieces. Put in a bowl. Rub with ½ teaspoon of the salt and the lemon juice.

Step Two Put the natural yoghurt into a separate small bowl. Add the chickpea flour and mix well. Now add the remaining salt, the ginger, garlic, chilli powder, turmeric, cumin and garam masala. Mix well and pour over the chicken pieces. Mix well again and set aside for 15 minutes or longer (you could even leave it overnight).

Step Three Preheat the grill. Thread the chicken pieces on to 4 skewers and balance the skewers on the raised edges of a grill rack. You could, as an alternative, spread the chicken pieces out on the grilling tray. Baste with the melted butter or oil. Grill the chicken pieces about 10cm (4in) from the source of heat for 5 minutes, basting once during this time. Turn the chicken pieces over, baste again and grill for 2–3 minutes or until just cooked through. Serve immediately.

Chicken in a Spinach and Mustard Sauce

I was trying to work out a quick version of seasoning a chicken dish with crushed mustard seeds and vinegar when it occurred to me that I could just use a grainy mustard. This particular mustard is labelled Moutarde de Meaux or Pommery. Any grainy French mustard will do.

Step One Cut the chicken into serving portions (a pair of breasts into 4–6 pieces each, whole legs into 2–3 pieces each). Put 4 tablespoons oil in a large, wide, non-stick pan (a large, non-stick frying pan is also quite suitable) and set over a medium–high heat. When hot, put in the bay leaves, cardamon pods, cinnamon stick, cloves and red chillies. Stir for a few seconds or until the bay leaves turn a few shades darker. Now put in the chicken pieces and brown well on both sides. Add the sultanas and stir for a few seconds. Add the yoghurt, 1 teaspoon salt, lots of freshly ground black pepper and the chilli powder. Stir and bring to a simmer. Cover well, turn the heat to low and simmer gently for 15 minutes.

Step Two While the chicken simmers, put the ginger into the container of a blender along with 3 tablespoons water and blend until you have a smooth paste. Add the green chillies and a generous fistful of green coriander and continue to blend, pushing down with a rubber spatula when necessary. Now add the lightly drained spinach. Blend very briefly this time. The spinach should have a coarse texture and should not be a fine purée. Empty this green sauce into a bowl. Add the mustard and ¼ teaspoon salt. Mix.

Step Three When the chicken has cooked for 15 minutes, remove the cover and add the green sauce. Stir to mix. Bring to a simmer, cover again and cook for about 10 minutes or until the chicken is tender. Turn the chicken pieces a few times during this period.

Note

The large whole spices are not meant to be eaten.

Serves 3–4

vegetable oil

3 bay leaves

6 cardamom pods

5cm (2in) cinnamon stick

5 cloves

2 dried hot red chillies

1kg (2¼ lb) chicken pieces, skinned

4 tablespoons sultanas

6 tablespoons natural yoghurt

salt and freshly ground black pepper

⅛–¼ teaspoon chilli powder

5cm (2in) piece fresh ginger, peeled and chopped

1–2 fresh hot green chillies, sliced into coarse rings

green coriander tops

275g (10oz) frozen, chopped spinach, boiled until defrosted then lightly drained

3 tablespoons Pommery mustard

Cardamom and Black Pepper Chicken

To slice the chicken breasts evenly, it is best if you freeze them in a single layer for 35–45 minutes first. When they are half-frozen and firm, it is easy to cut them uniformly.

Serves 4

for the marinade

6 tablespoons onion,

5cm (2in) piece fresh ginger

2 large garlic cloves,

salt

cayenne pepper

freshly ground black pepper

450 (1lb) boned and skinned chicken breasts

to cook the chicken

150g (5oz) onions

corn or olive oil

1 medium stick cinnamon

8 whole cardamom pods

½ teaspoon ground cumin

½ teaspoon ground coriander

4 tablespoons natural yoghurt

5 tablespoons tomato, grated

1 teaspoon salt

¼ teaspoon garam masala

2–3 teaspoons lemon juice

Step One To make the marinade, peel and finely chop the onion, ginger and garlic and put them into a blender with ½ teaspoon salt, ½ teaspoon cayenne pepper, ½ teaspoon black pepper and 3 tablespoons water. Blend to a smooth paste, pushing down with a rubber spatula when needed. Cut the chicken breasts crossways into 3mm (⅛in thick) slices and put in a bowl. Add the marinade and mix well. Cover and refrigerate for 30 minutes, or up to 3 hours if desired.

Step Two Peel the onions and slice into fine half-rings. Pour 3 tablespoons oil into a wide, non-stick pan set over a medium–high heat. When the oil is hot, add the cinnamon stick and cardamom pods. Stir for 10 seconds, then add the onions and fry, stirring at the same time, for 6–7 minutes or until the onion turns a reddish-brown colour. Add the cumin and coriander. Stir once. Add the natural yoghurt, a tablespoon at a time, and stir until it is absorbed. Add the tomato and stir for a minute.

Step Three Reduce the heat to medium, add the chicken, together with its marinade, and cook, stirring, for 3–4 minutes or until all the chicken pieces turn white. Add 175ml (6fl oz) water, the salt, garam masala and lemon juice. Stir and bring to a simmer. Reduce the heat to low and cook, uncovered, for 2–3 minutes, stirring now and then.

Note

The large, whole spices are not meant to be eaten.

Royal Chicken Cooked in Yoghurt

An elegant dish that may be served to the family or at a grand party. Rice is the ideal accompaniment.

Step One Put the natural yoghurt into a bowl and beat it lightly until it is smooth and creamy. Add half the salt, some black pepper, the ground cumin, ground coriander, chilli powder and green coriander. Mix and set aside.

Step Two Salt and pepper the chicken pieces on both sides using the remaining ½ teaspoon salt. Put the oil in a wide, preferably non-stick pan and set over medium–high heat. When hot, put in the cardamom pods, cloves, cinnamon stick and bay leaves. Stir once and add some of the chicken pieces – only as many as the pan will hold easily in a single layer. Brown on both sides and remove to a large bowl. Brown all the chicken pieces in this way and remove to the bowl.

Step Three Put the almonds and sultanas into the same hot oil. Stir quickly. The almonds should turn golden and the sultanas should plump up – which will happen very fast. Now return the chicken and its accumulated juices to the pan. Add the seasoned natural yoghurt. Stir to mix and bring to a simmer. Cover, turn the heat to low and simmer gently for 20 minutes, stirring once or twice during this period. Remove the cover, turn the heat up a bit and reduce the sauce until it is thick and just clings to the chicken pieces. Turn the chicken pieces over gently as you do this.

Note

The large, whole spices are not meant to be eaten.

Serves 4

250ml (8fl oz) natural yoghurt

1 teaspoon salt

freshly ground black pepper

1 teaspoon ground cumin

1 teaspoon ground coriander

¼ teaspoon chilli powder, or to taste

4 tablespoons finely chopped green coriander

1.5 kg (3lb) chicken, cut into serving portions

4 tablespoons vegetable oil

8 cardamom pods

6 cloves

5cm (2in) cinnamon stick

3 bay leaves

2½ tablespoons blanched, slivered almonds

2½ tablespoons sultanas

Silken Chicken 'Tikka' Kebabs (Reshmi Tikka Kebab)

These kebabs are very easy to prepare and have a delicate, delicious flavour.

Serves 4 as a main course, 8 as a starter

675g (1½ lb) boned and skinned chicken breasts, cut into 2½ cm (1in) pieces

1¼ teaspoons salt

3 tablespoons lemon juice

1 tablespoon peeled and very finely grated fresh ginger

2 garlic cloves, peeled and crushed to a pulp

1 teaspoon ground cumin

1 teaspoon bright red paprika

½–¾ teaspoon cayenne pepper

6 tablespoons whipping cream

½ teaspoon garam masala

3 tablespoons corn oil or peanut oil

Step One Put the chicken in a bowl. Add the salt and lemon juice and rub them in. Prod the chicken pieces lightly with the tip of a knife and rub the seasonings in again. Set aside for 20 minutes. Then add the ginger, garlic, cumin, paprika, cayenne pepper, cream and garam masala. Mix well, cover, and refrigerate for 6–8 hours. (Longer will not hurt.)

Step Two Just before serving, preheat the grill. Thread the chicken pieces onto two to four skewers (the flat, sword-like ones are best.) Brush with oil and balance the skewers on the rim of a shallow baking tray. Place about 13cm (5in) from the source of heat and grill for about 6 minutes on each side or until lightly browned and cooked through.

For more recipes from My Kitchen Table, sign up for our newsletter at www.mykitchentable.co.uk/newsletter

Sweet and Sour Chicken 'Rizala'

There is more than one style of rizala. The Dhaka rizala is neither sweet nor sour and is often served at the end of the Ramadan festival of Id. The Calcutta rizala requires that the meat be cooked entirely in milk or natural yoghurt. This north Bengali Bogra rizala recipe comes from my friend Yasmeen's mother. It is a classic. Gently sweet and sour, it has a scrumptious dark sauce made entirely without spices that is rich with browned onions and natural yoghurt. Note that the chillies do not give much heat to the dish. They may, however, be bitten into if the diner desires.

Step One Pour enough oil into a large frying pan to come to a depth of 3mm (⅛ in), and set over medium heat. When the oil is hot put in the onions and fry for about 8 minutes. The onions will have begun to brown. Reduce the heat to medium–low. Stir and fry for another 2 minutes or so. Reduce the heat to low. Continue to stir and fry until most of the slices are reddish-brown – about 12 minutes. Empty the frying pan contents into a sieve set over a bowl. Spread out the onions on kitchen paper to dry. Once completely cool, crumble the fried onions and set aside.

Step Two Peel and chop the onions, ginger and garlic and put them into a blender with 3–4 tablespoons water. Blend, pushing down with a rubber spatula when necessary, until you have a smooth paste.

Step Three Put the oil and ghee in a large, non-stick, lidded pan and set over a medium–high heat. When hot, pour in the paste from the blender. Stir and fry for about 5 minutes or until the paste is lightly browned. Add the chicken pieces. Continue to stir for a further minute. Over the next 5 minutes add 1 tablespoon of natural yoghurt at a time and keep browning the chicken. Now add 175ml (6fl oz) water, the crumbled onions and salt. Stir to mix and bring to a simmer. Cover, reduce the heat to very low and simmer gently for 20 minutes, turning the chicken pieces over now and then. Add the chillies, sugar and lemon or lime juice. Stir to mix. Cover and continue to cook on a very low heat for another 10 minutes.

Serves 4

3 small onions, each about 75g (3oz), peeled, cut in half lengthways and thinly sliced

corn or peanut oil

2 small onions, about 175g (6oz), peeled

5cm (2in) piece fresh ginger, peeled

4 garlic cloves, peeled

4 tablespoons oil saved from frying the onions, plus 1 tablespoon ghee, or more oil

1 chicken, about 1.75kg (4lb), skinned and cut into small serving pieces

6 tablespoons natural yoghurt

1½ teaspoons salt

6–10 whole bird's eye chillies, with small slits cut in them

1¾ teaspoons sugar

2 tablespoons lemon or lime juice

Duck Cooked in the Delhi Hunter's Style

During the winter months when my father and brothers went hunting, they usually came back with a lot of duck. It was then cooked in our kitchens with cinnamon and nutmeg. I like to cook the duck a day before I serve it so that I can remove all the fat that congeals at the top.

Serves 4

2 medium onions

6 medium garlic cloves, peeled

corn oil or peanut oil

a 2.7kg (6lb) duck, jointed and partially skinned

1 medium stick cinnamon

7 whole cardamom pods

2 bay leaves

2 tablespoons peeled and finely grated fresh ginger

½ teaspoon ground turmeric

1 tablespoon ground cumin

1 tablespoon paprika

1 tablespoon ground coriander

1 teaspoon cayenne pepper

1½ teaspoons garam masala

2 medium tomatoes

2 teaspoons salt

½ teaspoon ground cinnamon

¼ teaspoon freshly grated nutmeg

Step One Slice the onions into fine half-rings and crush the garlic cloves to a pulp. Pour 4 tablespoons of oil into a large, wide, lidded pan and set over a medium–high heat. When the oil is hot, put in as many duck pieces, skin-side down, as the pan will hold easily in a single layer. Lightly brown the duck, about 3–4 minutes per side, and remove to a bowl. Brown all the duck pieces this way and remove.

Step Two Add the cinnamon stick, cardamom pods and bay leaves to the hot fat and, 10 seconds later, add the onions. Stir and fry until the onions begin to turn brown at the edges. Now add the ginger and garlic. Stir and fry for a minute. Add the turmeric, cumin, paprika, coriander, cayenne pepper and garam masala. Stir for 30 seconds. Add the tomatoes, and cook until they have softened, about 2–3 minutes, stirring and scraping the bottom of the pan as you do this. Now add the browned duck pieces, the salt and 475ml (16fl oz) water. Stir and bring to the boil. Cover, reduce the heat to low, and cook gently for 1 hour and 15 minutes or until the duck is tender, lifting the lid to stir now and then.

Step Three Check for salt, adding more if needed. Add the cinnamon and nutmeg and continue to cook, stirring now and then, for a further 10 minutes. Remove as much fat as possible before serving.

Note

The large, whole spices are not meant to be eaten.

From Sameena at Yousaf Salahuddin's Home
Braised Quail (Bater)

This quail is often part of winter lunches served on sunny verandahs and courtyards of grand homes in Lahore. All the guests come bedecked in their winter finery, which for most of them (as with most north Indians), means exquisite Kashmiri shawls. The quail used here were wild and quite small.

Step One Put the ginger, garlic and chillies in a blender along with 4 tablespoons water and blend until smooth. Slice the onions into very fine half-rings. Grind the coriander seeds to a coarse powder. Finely grate the tomatoes.

Step Two Put the oil and butter in a large, wide, heavy-lidded pan and set over a medium–high heat. When hot, add the onions. Stir and fry, turning the heat down to medium as needed, until the onions are a medium brown. Add the ginger–garlic mixture. Stir and fry on a medium heat for 3–4 minutes. Add 250ml (8fl oz) water, as well as the cayenne pepper, coriander, salt, turmeric, tomatoes and natural yoghurt. Bring to the boil on a medium–high heat. Cook, stirring frequently, until the sauce is thick and the oil separates from it. Add the quail. Stir and fry for 3–4 minutes. Cover tightly, reduce the heat to low, and braise gently for 1 hour and 15 minutes or until the quail are tender. They should cook in their own juices. If they dry out, add a few tablespoons of water. Turn the birds around and stir gently every 6–7 minutes. Sprinkle over the garam masala 5 minutes before the cooking ends and stir it in.

Serves 4 as a main course, 8 as a starter

7.5cm (3in) piece fresh ginger, peeled and finely chopped

5 garlic cloves, peeled and chopped

2 fresh hot green chillies, chopped (if using a jalapeño, use 1, with its seeds)

2 medium onions

2 teaspoons whole coriander seeds

2½ medium tomatoes, peeled

3 tablespoons corn, peanut or olive oil

25g (1oz) unsalted butter

1 teaspoon cayenne pepper

1¼ teaspoons salt

¼ teaspoon ground turmeric

120ml (4fl oz) natural yoghurt, lightly beaten

8 quail

½ teaspoon garam masala

Lamb with Whole Spices and Onions

This is one of the first meat recipes I learned to cook. It is little changed from the original, passed on to me by my mother. When the meat is cooked, it should be nicely browned, and the only liquid should be the sauce clinging to it and the oil it is cooked in. In India, this is how the dish is served, but Westerners may be put off by the quantity of oil in the serving dish, so I suggest you lift out the meat and spices with a slotted spoon and transfer them to another dish. The spices serve as a garnish; they are not to be eaten.

Serves 4–6

900g (2lb) boneless shoulder of lamb, trimmed of fat

4 onions

4cm (1½ in) cube fresh ginger

9 tablespoons vegetable oil

10 whole green cardamom pods

4 whole large black cardamom pods (if available)

6–7 bay leaves

1 teaspoon cumin seeds

1–4 whole hot dried red peppers (optional)

5 black peppercorns

salt

Step One Cut the meat into 2½–4 cm (1–1½in) cubes and pat dry thoroughly with kitchen paper.

Step Two Peel the onions, cut in half, then slice thinly into half-circles. Peel and grate the ginger.

Step Three Heat the oil in a large, heavy-based cooking pot or flameproof casserole over a medium heat. When hot, add the onions and fry, stirring occasionally, for 15 minutes or until brown and crisp, but not burned. Lift out the onions with a slotted spoon and spread out on kitchen paper to drain.

Step Four Add all the cardamom pods, the bay leaves, cumin seeds, red peppers, peppercorns and the ginger to the oil remaining in the cooking pot. Stir for 1 minute until the bay leaves darken and the ginger is sizzling. Add the meat and ½–1 teaspoon salt. Cook, stirring, for about 5 minutes until the liquid begins to bubble vigorously. Cover, lower the heat and simmer very gently for 1 hour and 10 minutes or until the meat is tender.

Step Five Add the onions and cook, uncovered, over a medium heat for a final 3–5 minutes, stirring gently. Take care not to break up the meat. Any excess liquid should have boiled away, leaving the meat only with the sauce that clings to it, and the fat left in the pot. Serve as suggested above.

Minced Lamb with Tomatoes and Peas

Here I have used a quick method to chop the onion, garlic and ginger finely. I put them into a food processor and used the 'pulse' method rapidly starting and stopping the machine until I have the result I want.

Step One Coarsely chop the onions, ginger and garlic, then put them into the container of a food processor and chop finely.

Step Two Put 4 tablespoons oil in a wide, non-stick pan and set over a medium–high heat, When hot, put in the finely chopped mixture from the food processor. Stir and fry until it is somewhat brown. Add the chilli powder, cumin seeds, coriander seeds and turmeric. Stir once or twice. Now add the tomatoes and natural yoghurt. Stir on high heat until the tomatoes are soft. Add the meat, salt and garam masala. Stir, breaking up any lumps, for 2 minutes. Add 250ml (8fl oz) water. Stir and bring to a simmer. Cover, turn the heat to low and simmer for 25 minutes.

Step Three Add the lemon juice, green chilli, green coriander and peas. Stir and bring to a simmer. Cover the pan and cook on low heat for 10 minutes.

Serves 4–6

115g (4oz) onions, peeled

5cm (2in) piece fresh ginger, peeled

5–6 large garlic cloves, peeled

vegetable oil

½ teaspoon chilli powder

1 teaspoon cumin seeds

1 teaspoon coriander seeds

½ teaspoon turmeric powder

200g (7oz) tomatoes, chopped

4 tablespoons natural yoghurt

550 g (1¼ lb) minced lamb

1¼ teaspoons salt

2 teaspoons garam masala

2 tablespoons lemon juice

1 fresh hot green chilli, chopped

6 tablespoons coarsely chopped green coriander

150g (5oz) peas, fresh or frozen

KITCHEN TABLE

For more recipes from My Kitchen Table, sign up for our newsletter at www.mykitchentable.co.uk /newsletter

Lamb Stewed in Coconut Milk

This is a meal in itself: a kind of Indian Lancashire hotpot that requires only rice – or a good crusty bread – on the side. I always serve something green as well. The cooking time in a saucepan would be about 70 minutes and you would need to add 150ml (5fl oz) water before starting to cook.

Serves 4

vegetable oil

12 fresh curry leaves, if available, or 3 bay leaves

5cm (2in) cinnamon stick

6 cardamom pods

8 cloves

15 black peppercorns

75g (3oz) onions, peeled and chopped

675g (1½ lb) boned shoulder of lamb, cut into 4cm (1½ in) chunks

450g (1lb) potatoes, peeled and cut into 4cm (1½ in) chunks

2 medium carrots, peeled and cut into 3 pieces each

¼ teaspoon ground turmeric

1 tablespoon ground coriander

⅛ –½ teaspoon chilli powder

1–2 fresh, hot green chillies

1¼ teaspoons salt

1 x 400g (14oz) tin coconut milk

Step One Put 3 tablespoons oil in a pressure cooker and set over medium–high heat. When hot, put in the curry leaves, cinnamon stick, cardamom, cloves and peppercorns. Stir once and add the onions. Sauté for 1½ minutes or until the onions are soft. Add the meat, potatoes, carrots, turmeric, coriander, chilli powder, green chillies, salt and 250ml (8fl oz) of the well-stirred coconut milk. Cover securely with the lid and, on high heat, bring up to full pressure. Turn the heat to low and cook for 15 minutes. Lower the pressure with the help of cool water and remove the lid.

Step Two Cook, uncovered, over high heat for 5 minutes, stirring gently as you do this. Add the remaining coconut milk and bring to a simmer. Turn off the heat.

Lamb with Cardamom

Many versions of this dish exist among the Sindhi community of India. Here the green cardamom pods are ground whole, skin and all. This recipe comes from Draupadiji, a veritable treasure house of Sindhi specialities. The mild, aromatic dish – it has no red chillies – is very much like a stew; gentle and soothing. It should have quite a bit of sauce. Sindhis often eat it with bread, so serving it with a good, crusty loaf would be downright 'authentic'. You may serve a salad or a selection of Indian vegetables on the side. You do not, of course, have to use a pressure cooker here. If you use an ordinary saucepan, put in 600ml (1 pint) water and cook for 1 hour or a bit longer.

Step One Put the cardamom pods into the container of a clean coffee grinder or other spice grinder and grind until you have a fine powder.

Step Two Put the oil in a pressure cooker and set over a medium–high heat. When hot, put in the cardamom powder. Stir once and put in all the meat. Stir over high heat for 2 minutes. Add the tomatoes and onions, stirring for another 3 minutes. Now put in the garam masala, tomato purée, salt and 450ml (15fl oz) water. Cover tightly and bring up to pressure. Turn the heat to low and cook for 15 minutes. Reduce the pressure quickly with cool water and uncover.

Step Three Reheat the meat over high heat. Grind in a very generous amount of black pepper and cook, stirring gently, for a minute. Check the salt.

Serves 6

2 tablespoons cardamom pods (the green kind sold by Indian grocers are best)

3 tablespoons vegetable oil

900g (2lb) boned shoulder of lamb, cut into 2.5cm (1in) cubes

2 large tomatoes, chopped

4 tablespoons finely chopped onions (red onions or shallots are ideal, but any will do)

1½ teaspoons garam masala

1 tablespoon tomato purée

1½ teaspoons salt, or to taste

freshly ground black pepper

Lamb or Beef with Spinach

This is the classic dish, prepared in almost every north Indian home and loved by all. To make it quickly, a pressure cooker is essential. If you use a regular saucepan it will take about 1 hour for the lamb to cook and 1½ hours for beef. You will need to increase the amount of water to 600ml (1 pint).

Serves 4

275g (10oz) packet frozen, chopped spinach

275g (10oz) onions, peeled

5cm (2in) piece fresh ginger, peeled

6–8 garlic cloves, peeled

6 tablespoons vegetable oil

3 bay leaves

10 cardamom pods

8 cloves

2 x 5cm (2in) cinnamon sticks

675g (1½ lb) stewing beef or boned shoulder of lamb, cut into 4cm (1½ in) pieces

1⅓ teaspoons salt

1 tablespoon ground coriander

1 teaspoon ground cumin

¼–1 teaspoon chilli powder

1 teaspoon garam masala

Step One Drop the spinach into boiling water according to the instructions on the packet and boil just until it is defrosted. Drain and squeeze out most of the water.

Step Two Coarsely chop the onions and ginger and put into the container of a food processor. Add the garlic and 'pulse', starting and stopping with great rapidity, until finely chopped.

Step Three Put the oil in a pressure cooker and set over high heat. When hot, put in the bay leaves, cardamom pods, cloves and cinnamon sticks. Stir once or twice and put in the finely chopped seasonings from the food processor. Stir and cook over high heat for 5 minutes. Add the beef or lamb, the spinach, 450ml (15fl oz) water, salt, coriander, cumin and chilli powder. Stir. Cover, securing the pressure-cooker lid, and bring up to full pressure. The beef will take 20 minutes, the lamb 15 minutes.

Step Four Cool off the pressure cooker quickly with cool water and remove the lid. Put in the garam masala and bring the contents of the pressure cooker to a boil again. Cook, uncovered, stirring gently over high heat for about 7–10 minutes or until the sauce is reduced and thick. (Leave the oil behind, when serving.)

Note

The large, whole spices are not meant to be eaten.

Hyderabadi Lamb with Tomatoes

A light, simple dish that may be eaten with Indian breads or rice, but is also wonderful with all kinds of pasta, Asian or Italian.

Step One Put the meat in a bowl. Add the ginger, garlic, cumin, turmeric and 1 teaspoon of the salt. Mix well and set aside for 30 minutes. Pour the oil into a wide, non-stick, lidded pan and set over a medium–high heat. When hot, stir in the onions and fry them until the pieces turn brown at the edges.

Step Two Add the meat, together with its marinade. Stir and fry for 1 minute. Cover, reduce the heat to medium–low, and cook for 8–10 minutes, removing the lid now and then to stir the contents until the meat is lightly browned. Stir in the tomatoes, the remaining salt, the chillies, curry leaves and coriander, and bring to a simmer. Cover, reduce the heat to very low, and cook gently, stirring occasionally, for about 50 minutes or until the meat is tender.

Serves 4

560g (1lb) boneless lamb shoulder, cut into 2½ cm (1in) cubes

1 tablespoon fresh ginger, peeled and finely grated

6 garlic cloves, peeled and crushed to a pulp

1½ teaspoons ground cumin

½ teaspoon ground turmeric

1¼ teaspoons salt

3 tablespoons corn or peanut oil

210g (7½ oz) onion, peeled and finely chopped

450g (1lb) fresh tomatoes, peeled, finely chopped and crushed

3–6 fresh, hot green chillies, chopped

10–15 fresh curry leaves, if available (use fresh basil leaves as an interesting substitute)

2–3 tablespoons chopped fresh coriander

Rehana Saigol's Lamb Shanks Braised in a Yoghurt Sauce (Kunna)

This little-known dish consists of large pieces of meat that are braised very slowly in a clay pot buried in hot ashes and earth. The meat gets so tender, it practically falls off the bone. Since burying clay pots in hot ashes is beyond most of us, I have devised a method that cooks kunna slowly in an oven. You will need a non-stick pan that can be used in the oven. If you do not have one, use a heavy, non-stick roasting pan and cover it with a large piece of heavy-duty foil. I have allowed about half a shank per person.

Serves 6

3 lamb shanks, about 1.6–1.75kg (3¾–4lb)

salt and freshly ground black pepper

13cm (5in) piece fresh ginger

8 garlic cloves

4 tablespoons whole coriander seeds

475ml (16fl oz) natural yoghurt

olive or corn oil

2 teaspoons whole cumin seeds

1 teaspoon whole cloves

4 sticks cinnamon

2 teaspoons whole black peppercorns

2–3 teaspoons coarsely ground pure chilli powder or cayenne pepper

½ teaspoon ground turmeric

Step One Place the shanks in a single layer and sprinkle all over with ½ teaspoon salt and lots of black pepper. Pat them in.

Step Two Peel and coarsely chop the ginger and garlic. Put in a blender with 4 tablespoons water and blend until smooth. Set aside. Put the coriander seeds in a clean coffee grinder and grind coarsely. You may use a mortar and pestle for this instead. Set aside. Lightly beat the natural yoghurt. Set aside.

Step Three Preheat the oven to 160°C/325° F/gas mark 3. Pour 8 tablespoons oil into a wide, non-stick, lidded pan and set over a high heat. When hot, add the lamb shanks and brown lightly on all sides. Remove. Quickly add the cumin, cloves, cinnamon and peppercorns to the hot oil in the pan. Ten seconds later, add the ginger–garlic paste, stir, and fry for 5–6 minutes or until lightly browned. Take the pan off the heat and add the beaten natural yoghurt and 475ml (16fl oz) water. Stir well. Return to the heat, add the coarsely ground coriander, chilli powder, turmeric and 1½ teaspoons salt, and stir to mix. Put the lamb shanks back into the pan, spoon some sauce over them, and bring to the boil. Cover well, first with foil, crimping the edges, then with the lid, place in the oven and bake slowly for 3 hours, turning the shanks over every 30 minutes.

Step Four Remove the pan from the oven and uncover. Set over a high heat and reduce the liquid, basting the shanks as you do so, until you have a thick sauce, about 6–7 minutes.

Pork or Lamb 'Vindaloo'

The main ingredients for this Portuguese-inspired Indian dish are wine vinegar and garlic. Additions of mustard seeds, cumin, turmeric and chillies make it specifically colonial Goan. Most recipes for vindaloo involve grinding mustard seeds in vinegar. To save this step, I have used grainy French Pommery mustard (Moutarde de Meaux) which already contains vinegar. It works beautifully. This dish may be made in the pressure cooker or in a frying pan. Vindaloos are hot. Goans would use 4 teaspoons of chilli powder here. Under my husband's 'spare-me' gaze, I have used half a teaspoon to make a mild dish. It is up to you.

Step One Combine the mustard, cumin, turmeric, chilli powder, salt and vinegar in a cup. Mix well.

Step Two Slice the onions into fine half-rings and crush the garlic to a pulp. Put the oil in a large, non-stick frying pan and set over medium–high heat. When hot, add the onions. Stir and fry until they are medium brown. Add the garlic. Stir and fry for 30 seconds. Add the paste from the cup. Stir and fry for a minute, then add the meat. Stir and fry for about 3 minutes.

Step Three Now add in the coconut milk and 150ml (5fl oz) water if you are going to cook in a pressure cooker and 250ml (8fl oz) water if you are going to continue to cook in the frying pan. (Transfer to a pressure cooker at this stage if that is your intention.) Cover and either bring up to pressure, or to a boil if you are using the frying pan. Lower the heat to a simmer and cook for 20 minutes in a pressure cooker and 60–70 minutes in the frying pan.

Serves 3–4

1½ tablespoons grainy French mustard (see above)

1½ teaspoons ground cumin

¼ teaspoon ground turmeric

½–1 teaspoon chilli powder

1 teaspoon salt

1 teaspoon red wine vinegar

100g (4oz) onions, peeled

6 large garlic cloves, peeled

3 tablespoons vegetable oil

550g (1¼ lb) boned hand of pork or shoulder of lamb, cut into 2.5cm (1in) cubes

150ml (5fl oz) tinned coconut milk, well stirred

Pork Chops à la Jaffrey

I apologise for this name. The dish is really my very own concoction and unlikely to be served in any Indian home other than mine. Indians almost never use celery in their cooking. Nor do they often use soy sauce, though I must say that in the major cities the influence of an overcooked version of Chinese cuisine is certainly making itself felt. This recipe acknowledges its debt to that cuisine, but tastes, in the last analysis, rather Indian.

Serves 2

4 pork chops (loin or rib)

2 tablespoons vegetable oil

2 bay leaves

1 hot dried red pepper (optional)

8 whole cloves

1 large stick celery, diced

1 medium-sized onion, coarsely chopped

1 piece fresh ginger, 2.5cm (1in) long and 1cm (½in) wide, sliced into 3 rounds

2 garlic cloves, peeled

⅛ teaspoon ground cinnamon

⅛ teaspoon ground mace

3 tablespoons soy sauce

1½ teaspoons sugar

½ lemon

Step One Try to get pork chops that are evenly cut, so that they may brown evenly. Pat the chops dry and trim all but 0.5cm (¼in) of the fat. Place them in a large frying pan and turn heat on high. The chops should brown in their own fat. When they are a golden colour on both sides (press down areas that refuse to touch the frying pan), remove them from the frying pan and place in a bowl or on a plate. Turn off the heat and pour off only the accumulated fat in the frying pan.

Step Two Heat the vegetable oil along with the coagulated juices in the same frying pan over a medium heat, and put in the bay leaves, red pepper and cloves. Stir. When the bay leaves change colour (this should take a few seconds) add the celery, onion, ginger and garlic. Stirring, fry over medium flame for 4–5 minutes or until everything is slightly browned. Add the browned pork chops, cinnamon, mace, soy sauce, sugar and 50ml (2fl oz) water. Cut the lemon into 4 round slices (skin and all – remove any pips, though) and place over the chops. Bring to the boil. Cover, lower the heat, and simmer gently 50 minutes to 1 hour or until tender. Turn and mix gently every 10 to 15 minutes.

Step Three To serve, place the contents of the frying pan on a platter and serve with Plain Basmati Rice (see page 172) and a green salad. A natural yoghurt type of relish would be a good side dish. If you like, you can remove the pieces of ginger and garlic before you serve.

Pork in a Mustard Spice Mix

The flavour in this curry sauce comes from both the ground mustard in the spice mix and the whole mustard seeds that have been popped in hot oil. I love to serve this with dark, leafy greens and rice.

Step One First make the mustard spice mix. Put all the spices in a medium, cast-iron frying pan and set over medium heat. Stir and fry until the spices are just a shade darker and emit a roasted aroma. Empty the spices into a bowl or on to kitchen paper and allow to cool. Then put them into a clean coffee grinder or other spice grinder and grind as finely as possible. These quantities make more than you need for this recipe but you can store the spice mix in a tightly lidded jar, away from sunlight and moisture, for use in other recipes.

Step Two Rub the pork cubes well with the ginger, garlic, salt and turmeric. Cover and set aside for 30 minutes, or up to 8 hours if desired, refrigerating if necessary.

Step Three Pour the oil into a large, preferably non-stick, lidded pan and set over a medium–high heat. When the oil is hot, put in the whole mustard seeds. As soon as they pop, which will be in a matter of seconds, add the curry leaves and, a second later, the pork, together with its marinade. Stir for a minute. Cover, reduce the heat to medium, and let the meat cook for the next 5 minutes, stirring now and then and replacing the cover each time. The meat should brown lightly. Add 5 teaspoons of the mustard spice mix and stir for a minute. Add the tomatoes and cook, stirring, until the tomatoes turn pulpy, about 2 minutes. Now add 250ml (8fl oz) water, stir, and bring to the boil. Cover, reduce the heat, and cook very gently, lifting the lid occasionally to stir the contents, for 50–60 minutes or until the meat is tender. Check for salt before serving.

Serves 4

for the mustard spice mix

2 tablespoons whole coriander seeds

1 teaspoon whole cumin seeds

1 teaspoon whole fenugreek seeds

1 teaspoon whole brown mustard seeds

1 teaspoon whole black peppercorns

2 whole, dried, hot red chillies

5 whole cloves

for the pork

550g (1¼ lb) boneless pork shoulder, cut into 2½ cm (1in) cubes

1 tablespoon fresh ginger, peeled and finely grated

6 garlic cloves, peeled and crushed to a pulp

1¼ teaspoons salt

¼ teaspoon ground turmeric

3 tablespoons corn oil or peanut oil

½ teaspoon whole mustard seeds

15–20 fresh curry leaves, if available

255g (8oz) tomatoes, peeled and finely chopped

For a video masterclass on marinating meat, go to
www.mykitchentable.co.uk /videos/marinatingmeat

Goan Pork with Potatoes

You may well call this a simple vindaloo. It has the pork, the garlic, the chillies and the vinegar, but all in gentle proportions. It is a superb dish that is best enjoyed with plain rice. I like to use small red potatoes here, though any waxy potato will do.

Serves 4

150g (5oz) onions

5 garlic cloves

2½ cm (1in) piece fresh ginger

2 teaspoons whole brown mustard seeds

1 teaspoon whole cumin seeds

2 teaspoons whole coriander seeds

3 whole cloves

2 tablespoons cider vinegar

¾–1 teaspoon cayenne pepper

2 teaspoons bright red paprika

salt and freshly ground black pepper

½ teaspoon ground turmeric

550g (1¼ lb) boneless pork shoulder, cut into 2½ cm (1in) cubes

corn oil or peanut oil

350g (12oz) waxy red potatoes, peeled and cut into 2½ cm (1in) chunks

½ teaspoon sugar

Step One Peel and chop the onions, garlic and ginger. Put half the mustard seeds and all the cumin seeds, coriander seeds and cloves in a clean coffee grinder or other spice grinder and grind as finely as possible. Put this spice mixture, as well as the onions, garlic, ginger, vinegar, cayenne pepper, paprika and 3 tablespoons of water into a blender. Blend until smooth.

Step Two Rub 1¼ teaspoons salt, ½ teaspoon black pepper, all the turmeric, and 2 tablespoons of the spice paste from the blender all over the pork pieces. Put in a plastic bag and refrigerate for at least 30 minutes, longer if desired.

Step Three Pour 3 tablespoons oil into a large, heavy, non-stick, lidded pan and set over a medium–high heat. When the oil is hot, add the remaining mustard seeds. As soon as they pop, which will be in a matter of seconds, add the remaining spice paste. Stir and fry for 5–6 minutes or until the paste is lightly browned. Add the pork, together with its marinade. Stir for a minute. Cover and reduce the heat to medium. Let the meat cook for about 10 minutes, lifting the lid now and then to stir. The meat should get lightly browned.

Step Four Add 700ml (1¼ pints) water, the potatoes, ½ teaspoon salt and the sugar. Stir and bring to the boil. Cover, reduce the heat to low, and cook very gently for 50–60 minutes or until the meat is tender.

Sri Lankan Curry with Coriander

Pandanus leaves may be bought in frozen packets from Indian and South-East Asian grocers.

Step One Put 2 teaspoons mustard seeds, ½ teaspoon peppercorns, 3 tablespoons coriander seeds and 2 cloves into a clean coffee grinder or other spice grinder. Grind as finely as possible. Chop the shallots, ginger, garlic and coriander and put them into a blender along with the chilli and 5 tablespoons water. Blend, pushing down as many times as needed with a rubber spatula, until you have a smooth purée.

Step Two Pour 3 tablespoons oil into a large, non-stick, lidded pan and set over a medium–high heat. When the oil is hot, add the cinnamon, cardamom pods, curry leaves and pandanus leaf. Stir for 5 seconds, then add the meat. Stir and fry until the meat is browned on all sides. Reduce the heat to medium and add the spice mixture from the coffee grinder. Stir for a minute. Now add the mixture from the blender. Stir and fry for 5 minutes. Add 600ml (1 pint) water, ½ teaspoon turmeric, lemon juice and salt. Stir to mix and bring to a simmer. Cover and cook on a very low heat for about 1 hour 20 minutes for beef, 60–80 minutes for lamb and pork. Stir once or twice during this period.

Step Three Add the coconut milk and heat through. Check for salt, adding a bit more if needed.

Serves 4

whole brown mustard seeds

whole peppercorns

whole coriander seeds

cloves

50g (2oz) shallots

1cm (½in) piece fresh ginger, peeled

3 medium garlic cloves, peeled

25g (1oz) fresh coriander

1–2 fresh, hot green chillies, sliced

corn oil or peanut oil

1 medium stick cinnamon

2 whole cardamom pods

10–15 fresh curry leaves, if available

5cm (2in) length fresh or frozen pandanus leaf

450g (1lb) stewing beef, pork or lamb, cut into 2½ cm (1in) pieces

ground turmeric

1 teaspoon fresh lemon juice

¾–1 teaspoon salt

250ml (8fl oz) coconut milk, shaken

Smothered Lamb (or Pork or Beef)

There may be a fair number of ingredients in this dish, but they all go into the pan at almost the same time so the preparation is quite painless. The taste, however, is scrumptious.

Serves 3–4

450g (1lb) boned shoulder of lamb or pork shoulder or stewing beef, cut into 2.5cm (1in) cubes

100g (4oz) onions

2.5cm (1in) piece fresh ginger

150g (5oz) tomatoes, skinned

1–2 fresh, hot green chillies

about ½ teacup finely chopped green coriander

¼ teaspoon ground turmeric

2 teaspoons garam masala

1 teaspoon ground cumin

4 tablespoons natural yoghurt

1 tablespoon tomato purée

¼ teaspoon salt, or to taste

vegetable oil

4 garlic cloves, peeled and finely chopped

freshly ground black pepper

Step One Peel and finely chop the onions and ginger. Finely chop the tomatoes and slice the chillies into fine rings. Put all the ingredients except the oil, garlic and black pepper into a bowl and mix well.

Step Two Put 3 tablespoons oil in a pressure cooker and set over medium–high heat. If you do not wish to use a pressure cooker, this dish may just as easily be cooked in a regular saucepan, though it will take longer. When the cooker or pan is hot, put in the garlic. Stir until the garlic pieces turn medium brown. Now add the seasoned meat and stir once or twice. Turn the heat to medium. Cover the pressure cooker tightly and bring up to pressure slowly. Cook lamb and pork for 15 minutes and beef for 20 minutes at full pressure. Reduce the pressure quickly with the help of cool water. Uncover. Cook, uncovered, over high heat until the sauce is thick, stirring gently as you do so. Sprinkle in lots of black pepper and stir again. If using a saucepan you will need to add about 300ml (10fl oz) water to the pan just before you begin the simmering. It will take anywhere from 1 to 1½ hours (the longer time for beef).

'Hamburger' Kebabs

These kebabs are utterly delicious and can be prepared – from start to finish – in as little as 15 minutes. They are meant to be very spicy. I have used just two green chillies but you could use one whole chilli per kebab if you are up to it. The kebabs may be eaten with rice and vegetables, but are best cut in halves and rolled up in a flat bread – such as a store-bought pitta or chapati or naan – along with a little salad and either some Fresh Green Mango Chutney (see page 195) or Fresh Red Chutney with Almonds (see page 196). You could also eat them like a hamburger, in a hamburger bun. Again, a little salad and fresh chutney should be sandwiched in as well.

Step One Put the chickpea flour in a small cast-iron frying pan and stir around over medium heat until it has turned a light brown colour. Put it into a bowl, then add all the other ingredients except the oil and mix well.

Step Two Form 10 5cm (2in) balls. Flatten the balls to make 10 9cm (3½in) hamburger-like discs.

Step Three Just before eating, put 2 tablespoons of the oil into a large non-stick frying pan and set over a medium–high heat. When hot, put in as many kebabs as the pan will hold in a single layer. Turning them over every 30 seconds or so, cook the kebabs for about 2½ minutes or until they have browned on both sides. Remove to a warm plate. Use the remaining oil to cook a second batch the same way.

Serves 4–5

1 tablespoon chickpea flour (also called gram flour or besan)

675g (1½ lb) minced beef or lamb

6–7 tablespoons coarsely chopped green coriander

2 or more fresh hot green chillies, cut into fine rounds and chopped

1½ teaspoons cumin seeds

1½ teaspoons coriander seeds

1 teaspoon freshly ground black pepper

1¼ teaspoons salt

½ lightly beaten egg

3–4 tablespoons vegetable oil

Have you made this recipe? Tell us what you think at
www.mykitchentable.co.uk/blog

Beef or Lamb with Onion and Green Pepper

An Anglo-Indian speciality, this calls for leftovers of cooked roast meat. Sunday's roast was invariably turned into a delicious jhal firezi on Mondays by many a family in cities like Calcutta. Sliced green chillies may be added to this dish at the same time as the green pepper if you want it really hot. You may serve the dish with rice, potatoes or breads.

Serves 3–4

350g (12oz) cooked, boneless roast beef or roast lamb

freshly ground black pepper

chilli powder

ground cumin

ground coriander

ground turmeric

red wine vinegar

salt

vegetable oil

1 teaspoon cumin seeds

1 teaspoon black or yellow mustard seeds

10 fenugreek seeds (optional)

100g (4oz) green pepper, de-seeded and cut lengthways into 3mm (⅛in) slivers

150g (5oz) onions, peeled and cut into fine half-rings

1 teaspoon Worcestershire sauce

Step One Cut the cooked meat into 5mm (¼in) slices. Now stack a few slices together at a time and cut into 5mm (¼in) slivers. This does not have to be done too evenly.

Step Two Combine 1 teaspoon black pepper, 1¼–1½ teaspoons chilli powder, 1 teaspoon cumin, 1 teaspoon coriander, 1 teaspoon turmeric, 1 teaspoon vinegar, ½ teaspoon salt and 2 tablespoons water in a small cup. Mix and set aside.

Step Three Put 3 tablespoons oil in a large frying pan over medium–high heat. When hot, add the cumin, mustard and fenugreek seeds. As soon as the mustard seeds begin to pop, add the green pepper and onions. Stir and fry until the onions have browned quite a bit and the mass of vegetables has reduced. Sprinkle about ⅛ teaspoon salt over the top and stir. Add the meat and the spice mixture from the cup. Stir rapidly on the same medium–high heat for a minute or so until the meat has heated through. Add the Worcestershire sauce and stir to mix.

Kheema with Fried Onions

This is easily my favourite kheema recipe. Nutmeg, mace and yoghurt are added to the meat for a slight variation. Peas can also be included if you like. Add 1 cup freshly shelled (or frozen) peas to the kheema 10 minutes before the end of the cooking time and continue to simmer for 5–10 minutes until the peas are tender. Serve with plain boiled rice, Moong Dal (see page 159) and a vegetable dish. This kheema is also excellent served with chapatis or pooris instead of rice.

Step One Peel the onions and finely chop two of them. Peel and finely chop the ginger. Peel and crush the garlic. Peel and chop the tomato. Halve and thinly slice the other onion into half-rings.

Step Two Heat the oil in a large, heavy-based frying pan over a medium heat. Add the sliced onion and fry for about 5 minutes until dark brown, but not burned. Remove with a slotted spoon and drain on kitchen paper; set aside. Add the bay leaves, cinnamon and cloves to the hot oil. When the bay leaves begin to darken and the cinnamon starts uncurling slightly, add the chopped onions, ginger and garlic. Fry, stirring, for 10–12 minutes, until the onions are browned. Lower the heat and add 1 tablespoon coriander, 1 tablespoon cumin and 1 tablespoon turmeric. Fry for about 1 minute, stirring all the time. Add the natural yoghurt and continue to cook, stirring, for 1 minute. Add the tomato to the pan and fry, stirring, for a further 2–3 minutes.

Step Three Add the meat, increasing the heat to medium (medium–high if the meat is watery). Fry, breaking up the lumps with the back of a slotted spoon, for about 7–8 minutes. Stir in ½ teaspoon mace, ½ teaspoon nutmeg, 1 teaspoon salt, ¼–½ teaspoon cayenne and 150ml (5fl oz) water. Bring to the boil, cover, lower the heat and simmer for 1 hour, stirring every 10 minutes or so. Stir in the browned onion and remove the cinnamon.

Serves 6

3 onions
2.5cm (1in) cube fresh ginger
5 garlic cloves
1 medium tomato
4 tablespoons vegetable oil
2 bay leaves
7.5cm (3in) stick cinnamon
6 cloves
ground coriander
ground cumin
ground turmeric
2 tablespoons natural yoghurt
900g (2lb) lean minced lamb or beef
ground mace
ground nutmeg
1 teaspoon salt
cayenne pepper (optional)

Ravi's Kerala-style 'Bhuna' Lamb, Pork, Beef or Veal (Kerala Ka Bhuna Gosht)

This dish is a great favourite in my sister's Delhi home, where it is prepared by her Malayali cook, who comes from Kerala in south-western India. You may use either stewing lamb or pork – ask your butcher for boneless meat from the shoulder – or boneless stewing veal. All these meats are eaten by the different religious groups in Kerala. Indeed, it is the only state where the sale of beef is perfectly legal. Serve with rice or flatbreads.

Serves 4–6

2 teaspoons whole cumin seeds

4 teaspoons whole coriander seeds

2 teaspoons whole mustard seeds

2–4 whole dried hot red chillies

2 teaspoons whole fennel seeds

2 teaspoons whole fenugreek seeds

corn oil or peanut oil

3 large shallots, about 150g (5oz)

4 cm (1½ in) piece fresh ginger

5–6 garlic cloves

10–15 fresh curry leaves, if available

2 medium tomatoes

900g (2lb) boneless lamb, pork shoulder or stewing veal or beef, cut into 3cm (1¼ in) pieces

salt

Step One Set a small or medium-sized cast-iron frying pan on a medium–high heat. When it is hot, put in the cumin seeds, coriander seeds, mustard seeds, chillies, fennel seeds and fenugreek seeds. Stir them around until they are a shade darker. Quickly empty them out and let them cool slightly. Now put them into a clean coffee grinder or other spice grinder and grind to a powder.

Step Two Peel and finely chop the shallots, ginger and garlic. Peel and chop the tomatoes. Pour 5 tablespoons oil into a wide, preferably non-stick, lidded pan and set over a medium–high heat. When the oil is hot, add the shallots, ginger and garlic. Fry, stirring at the same time, for 4–5 minutes until they turn a golden brown. Add the curry leaves and tomatoes. Cook, again stirring, until the tomatoes are reduced to a thick paste. Add the ground roasted spices. Stir into the paste and cook for a minute. Add the meat and 1¼–1½ teaspoons salt. Stir and cook for a further 5 minutes. Add 250ml (8fl oz) water and bring to a simmer. Cover tightly with the lid, reduce the heat to low, and simmer gently for about 80 minutes or until the meat is tender. (Beef will take about 1½ hours.) Remove the lid, increase the heat to high, and cook, stirring continuously, until the sauce is reduced to the point where it clings to the meat.

Red Beef Curry

The lovely red colour of this curry comes from rather a lot of chilli powder. I use a mix of cayenne pepper and paprika but you can change the proportions to suit yourself. If you cannot find ground fennel, you can grind the seeds yourself in a clean coffee grinder or other spice grinder.

Step One Put the meat in a bowl. Add 1 teaspoon each of ground coriander, cumin and fennel, ½–1 teaspoon cayenne pepper, 2 teaspoons paprika and lots of black pepper. Mix well to coat the beef and set aside for 15–20 minutes.

Step Two Peel and finely slice the shallots and garlic. Pour 3 tablespoons oil into a large, non-stick, lidded pan and set on a medium–high heat. When the oil is hot, add the cinnamon, 4 whole cardamom pods, ½ teaspoon fenugreek seeds, shallots, garlic, ginger, pandanus leaf and curry leaves. Stir for 2 minutes or until the onions have become translucent. Add the meat, and continue to stir for a further 2–3 minutes or until the meat is lightly browned. Add the salt, 350ml (12fl oz) water and the lemon juice, and bring to the boil. Cover, reduce the heat to very low, and simmer gently for 1 hour and 20 minutes or until the meat is tender. If the water dries out, just add a little bit more. Lift the lid to stir once or twice during this period.

Step Three Stir in the coconut milk and bring to a simmer. Taste for salt.

Serves 4

450g (1lb) stewing beef, cut into 2½cm (1in) pieces

ground coriander

ground cumin

ground fennel

cayenne pepper

bright red paprika

freshly ground black pepper

corn oil or peanut oil

1 medium stick cinnamon

cardamom pods

fenugreek seeds

4 tablespoons peeled and finely sliced shallots

2 garlic cloves

2 thin slices fresh ginger

5cm (2in) piece fresh or frozen pandanus leaf

10–15 fresh curry leaves, if available

¾ teaspoon salt

2 teaspoons lemon juice

175ml (6fl oz) shaken coconut milk

Beef 'Kaati' Kebab (Kaati Kabab)

Kaati kebabs are a Calcutta speciality and this is a simplified, Anglo-Indian version. It makes for a quick, easy meal. The kebabs are generally rolled into flatbreads along with thinly sliced raw onions and sliced green chillies, if liked, and eaten just as hamburgers might be. Sometimes the flatbread, say a paratha, is spread out on a hot, oiled griddle and an egg broken on it. The egg is spread around to cover the surface and then the paratha is flipped over briefly to allow the egg to cook through. This bread–egg combination is then used to wrap the meat. The meat is, of course, put on the egg side.

Serves 4

450g (1lb) well-marbled, boneless beef steaks, about 2cm (¾in) thick, cut into 2½cm (1in) pieces

1 tablespoon fresh ginger, peeled and very finely grated

4 garlic cloves, peeled and crushed to a pulp

½–1 teaspoon cayenne pepper

2 teaspoons ground coriander

¼ teaspoon ground turmeric

¾ teaspoon salt

freshly ground black pepper

2 tablespoons corn oil or peanut oil

Step One Put the steak pieces on a plate. Rub the seasonings, plus 1 tablespoon of the oil, all over the steak pieces, put in a plastic zip-lock bag and refrigerate for 4–6 hours.

Step Two Just before serving, set a large, cast-iron pan or griddle on a medium–high heat. Allow it to get very hot. Brush the pan with the remaining oil. Now put in the steak pieces in a single layer, doing two batches if necessary, and let them brown on one side. This will only take a minute or less. Turn and brown the other side. Now toss the pieces around for a minute. Serve immediately.

For more recipes from My Kitchen Table, sign up for our newsletter at www.mykitchentable.co.uk/newsletter

Aubergine Cooked with Crushed Mustard Seeds and Yoghurt

This quick-cooking dish from eastern India uses three ingredients that are very typical of Bengali cooking – mustard oil, panchphoran and crushed black mustard seeds.

Step One Discard the stem end of the aubergine and dice the aubergine into 2.5cm (1in) cubes.

Step Two Grind the mustard seeds lightly in a coffee grinder and then empty into a bowl. Add the cayenne and 250ml (8fl oz) water. Mix and set aside.

Step Three Heat the oil in a 30cm (12in) frying or sauté pan over a medium–high heat. When hot, put in the panchphoran. Stir the spices once. Immediately add the mustard seed mixture, the cubed aubergine and 1 teaspoon salt. Keep stirring and cooking until most of the liquid is absorbed. Add another 250ml (8fl oz) of water, cover, and turn the heat to low. Simmer gently for about 15 minutes or until the aubergine pieces are quite tender. Remove the cover and turn up the heat to boil off about half the liquid.

Step Four Just before serving, beat the yoghurt and ½ teaspoon salt with a fork until it becomes a smooth paste and pour over the aubergine. Heat through, but do not bring to the boil. Sprinkle black pepper and ground cardamom over the aubergine, stir and serve at once.

Serves 4

450–675g (1–1½ lb) aubergine

1½ tablespoon whole black mustard seeds

⅛ teaspoon cayenne pepper

7 tablespoons mustard oil or vegetable oil

1 tablespoon panchphoran

1½ teaspoons salt

250ml (8fl oz) natural yoghurt

⅛ teaspoon freshly ground black pepper

¼ teaspoon freshly ground cardamom seeds

Note

Panchphoran is a Bengali spice mixture consisting of fennel seeds, mustard seeds, fenugreek seeds, cumin seeds and kalongi (nigella seeds) mixed in equal proportion.

Green Beans with Fresh Coconut and Sesame Seeds

This is a very refreshing dish of green beans, quick and easy to make.

Serves 4

50g (2oz) freshly grated coconut (about 8 tablespoons)

4 tablespoons finely chopped fresh green coriander, or parsley

generous pinch of crushed asafoetida (optional)

½–1 fresh hot green chilli, finely chopped

½ teaspoon plus 1 tablespoon salt

450g (1lb) fresh green beans, trimmed and cut into 2.5cm (1in) lengths

6 tablespoons ghee or vegetable oil

2 tablespoons sesame seeds

1 tablespoon whole black mustard seeds

⅛–¼ teaspoon cayenne pepper (optional)

Step One Combine the coconut, coriander, asafoetida, green chilli and ¼ teaspoon salt in a bowl. Rub the mixture well with your hands. Set aside.

Step Two Add 1 tablespoon salt to 2 litres (3½ pints) water and bring to the boil in a large pot. Add the cut beans. Boil rapidly for 3 to 4 minutes or until beans are tender, but still bright green and crisp. Drain in a colander and refresh by moving the colander under cold running water. Set aside.

Step Three Heat the ghee or oil in a 25–30cm (10–12in) wide sauté pan or heavy pot over a medium heat. When hot, put in the sesame and mustard seeds. As soon as the mustard seeds begin to pop, add the cayenne pepper. Stir once and add the beans. Sauté the beans over medium–low heat for 1–2 minutes or until they are heated through and well coated with the seeds. Add ¼ teaspoon salt and stir. Now add the coconut–coriander mixture, stir once and remove from the heat. Serve immediately.

Gently Stewed Beetroots

Any beetroots may be used for this stew-like dish. My own favourite happens to be chioggia, a very early Italian variety. These beetroots are small and sweet, with radish-red skin and striated red and pale yellow flesh. I do not mean to sound like a garden catalogue, but these are certainly worth knowing about, if not growing. Mine are supplied by a local farmer.

Step One Peel the beetroots and cut them in 2.5cm (1in) chunks.

Step Two Put the oil in a wide, medium-sized pan and set over high heat. When hot, put in the cumin seeds and bay leaf. As soon as the bay leaf darkens slightly – this just takes seconds – add the tomatoes, cumin, coriander, turmeric, chilli powder, beetroots, salt and 350ml (12fl oz) water. Stir and bring to a boil. Cover, turn the heat to low and simmer for 30–40 minutes or until the beetroots are tender.

Serves 4–6

900g (2lb) raw beetroots without stems and leaves

3 tablespoons vegetable oil

1 teaspoon cumin seeds

1 bay leaf

250ml (8fl oz) tinned chopped tomatoes (or lightly drained tinned whole tomatoes)

1 teaspoon ground cumin

1 teaspoon ground coriander

¼ teaspoon ground turmeric

¼ teaspoon chilli powder

¼ teaspoon salt

Cabbage Stir-fried with Red Pepper Paste

Only the dark, outer leaves of the cabbage were originally included in this recipe, but I often add some of the inner cabbage together with a small amount of shrimp or anchovy paste.

Serves 4

450g (1lb) bok choi, other cabbage, cabbage greens or spring greens

100g (4oz) red pepper

50g (2oz) shallots or onions

2 large garlic cloves

½ teaspoon shrimp or anchovy paste (optional)

¼ teaspoon chilli powder

6 tablespoons vegetable oil

½ teaspoon salt

Step One Wash the cabbage leaves and drain. Stacking several of them together, cut them crossways into long, fine 3mm (⅛in) wide shreds.

Step Two Core and de-seed the red pepper, then chop coarsely. Peel and coarsely chop the shallots and garlic. Put the red pepper, shallots or onions, garlic, shrimp or anchovy paste, chilli powder and 3 tablespoons water in an electric blender. Blend until a coarse paste results – it should not be too smooth.

Step Three Set a wok over a high heat. When hot, add the oil. Once the oil is hot, put in the spice paste. Stir and fry for about 5 minutes or until the oil separates and the mixture is dark red in colour. Add the cabbage and salt and cook, stirring, for 30 seconds. Cover tightly, turn the heat to medium–low and cook for 8–10 minutes or until the cabbage is just cooked. (No water should be needed, but check after 5–6 minutes and add a little if the mixture appears dry.) Turn into a warmed dish and serve at once.

Village-style Carrots with Potatoes and Peas

A dish from the villages of the Punjab in north-western India, this is cooked up in open courtyards in the morning and then taken to the farmers in the fields at midday, along with breads, pickles and yoghurt or fresh buttermilk. In India, where the peas are much firmer, they are generally put in to cook at the same time as the carrots and potatoes. I have used frozen peas here. If you wish to use fresh peas, you could put them in with the carrots. However, if they seem very tender, put them in after the carrots and potatoes have cooked for 10 minutes.

Step One Put 3 tablespoons oil in a wide pan or a deep frying pan and set over medium–high heat. When hot, add the onion. Stir and fry for 4–5 minutes or until the onion starts to brown at the edges. Add the ginger and stir for 1 minute. Add the grated tomatoes, salt, cayenne, garam masala and turmeric. Stir and fry, still on medium–high heat, for 3–4 minutes or until the tomato mixture has thickened a bit. Now add the carrots and potatoes. Stir for 1 minute. Add 120ml (4fl oz) water and stir. Bring to a simmer. Cover, turn the heat to low and cook gently for 15–20 minutes or until the potatoes are tender. Add the peas, stir and cover again. Cook for a further 4–5 minutes or until the peas are cooked through. Serve hot.

Serves 6

vegetable oil

1 onion, peeled and finely chopped

2.5cm (1in) piece fresh ginger, peeled and cut into minute dice

2 medium tomatoes, weighing about 300g (11oz), grated

1¾–2 teaspoons salt

½–1 teaspoon cayenne pepper

2 teaspoons garam masala

¼ teaspoon ground turmeric

450g (1lb) carrots, peeled and cut into 1cm (½in) dice

450g (1lb) potatoes, peeled and cut into 1cm (½in) dice

165g (5½oz) frozen peas, defrosted

Cauliflower and Carrots with a Coconut Dressing

You may serve this dish hot, at room temperature, or cold, though I feel that it is best to mix the dressing in while the vegetables are still hot.

Serves 4

50g (2oz) fresh coconut or 25g (1oz) unsweetened desiccated coconut

425g (15oz) cauliflower florets

100g (4oz) carrots

50g (2oz) red pepper

1 garlic clove

4 teaspoons lime or lemon juice

1 teaspoon dark brown sugar

½ teaspoon chilli powder

salt

Step One If you are using fresh coconut, grate it finely. If using desiccated coconut, soak it in 4 tablespoons of boiling water for 30 minutes; most of the water will be absorbed.

Step Two Cut the cauliflower into slim, delicate florets – no wider than 2.5cm (1in), with stems no longer than 5cm (2in). Peel the carrots and cut into 5cm (2in) lengths. Quarter the thick pieces lengthways; halve the thinner pointed ends.

Step Three De-seed and coarsely chop the red pepper. Peel and chop the garlic. In an electric blender, combine the red pepper, garlic, lime or lemon juice, sugar, chilli powder and ½ teaspoon salt. Blend until smooth. Taste the dressing and add a little more salt if required.

Step Four Bring a large pan of salted water to a rolling boil. Add the cauliflower and carrots and boil rapidly for several minutes or until the vegetables are just tender but still retain a hint of crispness. Drain them quickly and turn into a serving bowl. Add the dressing and toss to mix. Sprinkle in the coconut and toss the vegetables again. Serve immediately or allow to cool.

For a video masterclass on chopping vegetables, go to
www.mykitchentable.co.uk/videos/choppingvegetables

my KITCHEN TABLE

Cauliflower and Aubergine Cooked in a Bengali Style

This warming and spicy dish will take the chill off autumn evenings. Serve with rice, a yoghurt relish and a bean dish.

Step One Put the mustard seeds in a clean spice or coffee grinder and grind to a fine powder. Empty into a small bowl. Add 175ml (6fl oz) water and set aside to soak for 20–30 minutes; do not stir.

Step Two Put vegetable oil, about 5cm (2in) deep, in a wok, deep frying pan or deep fryer and set over medium heat. When the oil is hot, put in the aubergines and deep-fry for about 8–10 minutes, until they are golden brown. Lift out with a slotted spoon and drain on kitchen paper. Turn the heat to medium–high to reheat the oil, then put in as many cauliflower florets as the pan will hold in a single layer. Fry until they are golden brown, about 2–3 minutes. Lift out with a slotted spoon and drain on kitchen paper. Fry all the florets. (The oil can be strained and re-used.)

Step Three Combine the turmeric, cayenne pepper and 2 tablespoons water in a small cup. Set this spice mixture aside.

Step Four Put the oil in a frying pan and set over medium heat. When very hot, put in the panchphoran. As soon as the mustard seeds in the panchphoran begin to pop – a matter of seconds – add the spice mixture. Stir once or twice. Carefully pour the watery top of the ground mustard seed mixture into the pan, making sure to leave all the thick paste behind (you do not need the thick paste). Add the aubergines, cauliflower, green chillies and salt. Stir to mix well. Bring to the boil. Cover, turn the heat to low and simmer for 3–4 minutes, or until there is only a small amount of liquid left at the bottom of the pan. Serve hot.

Serves 4–6

2 tablespoons brown mustard seeds

vegetable oil for deep-frying

4 small, slim Japanese or Italian aubergines, each weighing about 250g (9oz), halved lengthways and cut into 4-5cm (1½–2in) segments

1 large cauliflower, weighing about 800g (1¾lb), cut into delicate florets

½ teaspoon ground turmeric

½ teaspoon cayenne pepper

3 tablespoons mustard oil or any vegetable oil

1 teaspoon panchphoran (see *Note* below)

6 fresh green chillies

1¼ teaspoons salt

Note

Panchphoran is a Bengali spice mixture consisting of fennel seeds, mustard seeds, fenugreek seeds, cumin seeds and kalongi (*nigella seeds) mixed in equal proportion.*

Green Peas in a Creamy Sauce

This is a recipe where frozen peas can be used to great advantage. The sauce takes just minutes to put together and may be made up to a day in advance and refrigerated, if you so prefer. This dish may be served with all Indian meals. It also goes well with lamb and pork roasts.

Serves 5–6

¼ teaspoon sugar

½ teaspoon ground cumin

½ teaspoon garam masala

¼ teaspoon salt

¼ – ½ teaspoon chilli powder

1 tablespoon tomato purée

175ml (6fl oz) single cream

1 tablespoon lemon juice

2 tablespoons chopped green coriander

1 fresh hot green chilli, finely chopped

3 tablespoons vegetable oil

½ teaspoon cumin seeds

¼ teaspoon black or yellow mustard seeds

2 x 275g (10oz) packets frozen peas, defrosted under warm water and drained

Step One Combine the sugar, ground cumin, garam masala, salt, chilli powder and tomato purée. Slowly add 2 tablespoons water, mixing as you go. Add the cream slowly and mix. Add the lemon juice, green coriander and green chilli. Mix again and set this cream sauce aside.

Step Two Put the oil in a large frying pan and set over medium–high heat. When hot, put in the cumin and mustard seeds. As soon as the mustard seeds begin to pop – this just takes a few seconds – add the peas. Stir and fry the peas for 30 seconds, then add the cream sauce. Cook on high heat for about 1½–2 minutes or until the sauce has thickened, stirring gently as you do so.

Green Beans with Mushrooms

A hearty dish that may be served as part of an all-vegetarian meal or with any meat, poultry or fish.

Step One Put the oil in a wide pan and set over medium–high heat. When hot, add the cumin seeds. As soon as the seeds begin to sizzle, add the onion. Stir and fry until the onion browns. Add the ginger and garlic, stirring until the garlic starts to brown. Add the mushrooms. Stir and fry for 2 minutes. Add the beans, coriander, cumin, turmeric, garam masala, chilli powder, salt, tomato and 120ml (4fl oz) water. Bring to a boil. Cover, lower the heat and simmer for 15 minutes. Remove the cover, raise the heat and boil most of the liquid away, stirring gently as you do so.

Serves 4

5 tablespoons vegetable oil

¾ teaspoon cumin seeds

1 medium onion, peeled and cut into fine half-rings

2.5cm (1in) piece fresh ginger, peeled and cut into slivers

5 garlic cloves, peeled and chopped

225g (8oz) fresh mushrooms, thickly sliced

450g (1lb) green beans, trimmed and cut into 5cm (2in) segments

2 teaspoons ground coriander

1¼ teaspoons ground cumin

½ teaspoon ground turmeric

¾ teaspoon garam masala

¾ teaspoon chilli powder

1 teaspoon salt

1 medium tomato, coarsely chopped

Mushroom Curry

I have used ordinary white mushrooms here but you may make this with almost any seasonal mushrooms. Whichever kind you get, cut them into large, chunky pieces so they do not get lost in the sauce.

Serves 4

4cm (1½ in) piece fresh ginger, peeled and chopped

100g (4oz) onions, peeled and chopped

3 garlic cloves, peeled and chopped

450g (1lb) large mushrooms

6 tablespoons vegetable oil

3 tablespoons natural yoghurt

1 teaspoon tomato purée

2 teaspoons ground coriander

¼ teaspoon salt

⅛–¼ teaspoon chilli powder

2 tablespoons chopped green coriander

Step One Put the ginger, onion and garlic into the container of an electric blender along with 3 tablespoons water and blend until smooth. Wipe the mushrooms with a damp cloth and cut them into halves or quarters, depending upon size.

Step Two Put 3 tablespoons of the oil in a non-stick frying pan and set over high heat. When hot, put in the mushrooms. Stir and fry for 2–3 minutes or until the mushrooms have lost their raw look. Empty the contents of the pan into a bowl. Wipe the pan.

Step Three Put the remaining oil into the pan and set over high heat. When hot, add the paste from the blender. Stir and fry for 3–4 minutes until it starts turning brown. Add 1 tablespoon of the yoghurt and fry for 30 seconds. Add another tablespoon of the yoghurt and fry for 30 seconds. Do this a third time. Now add the tomato purée and fry for 30 seconds. Add the ground coriander and stir once or twice. Now put in 300ml (10fl oz) water, the mushrooms and their juices, salt and chilli powder. Stir and bring to a simmer. Turn the heat to low and simmer for 5 minutes. Sprinkle the green coriander over the top before serving.

New Potatoes with Cumin

Here is one of my favourite ways of preparing new potatoes, Indian-style. You may serve them with an Indian meal or, if you like, with Western dishes – anything from roasts to sausages. They are particularly good with my 'Hamburger' Kebabs (see page 107).

Step One Scrub the potatoes and put them in a saucepan. Cover with water to come about 2.5cm (1in) above the potatoes. Add 1 tablespoon salt to the water and bring to a boil. Cover. Boil until the potatoes are just tender. Drain and peel.

Step Two Put the oil in a large frying pan and set over medium–high heat. When hot, add the cumin seeds. Let the seeds sizzle for a few seconds. Now add the potatoes. Turn the heat down to medium. Brown the potatoes lightly on all sides. Turn the heat to low and add ¼ teaspoon salt and the ground cumin, garam masala and chilli powder. Cook, stirring, for a minute. Add the green coriander just before serving and toss to mix.

Serves 4–6

900g (2lb) new potatoes

salt

2½ tablespoons vegetable oil

1 teaspoon cumin seeds

1 teaspoon ground cumin

½ teaspoon garam masala

⅛–¼ teaspoon chilli powder

2–3 tablespoons chopped green coriander

Diced Potatoes with Spinach

All over north India, potatoes are cooked with greens. Fenugreek greens are preferred, but spinach makes a good alternative.

Serves 6

5–6 medium-sized waxy potatoes, about 900g (2lb)

1 tablespoon plus 1 teaspoon salt

450g (1lb) fresh or 1 packet frozen leaf spinach

6 tablespoons vegetable oil or ghee

½ teaspoon whole black mustard seeds

1 large onion, 75–90g (3–3½ oz), peeled and chopped

2 garlic cloves, peeled and finely chopped

1 teaspoon garam masala

1/16–1/8 teaspoon cayenne pepper (optional)

Step One Bring 1.5 litres (2½ pints) of water to the boil. Peel the potatoes and dice into 2cm (¼in) cubes, then add to boiling water with 1 tablespoon salt. Bring to the boil again. Cover, turn the heat to low and cook the potatoes until they are just tender – about 6 minutes. Do not overcook. Drain. Spread the potatoes out and leave them to cool.

Step Two If using fresh spinach, wash carefully and drop into large pan of boiling water to wilt. Drain. Squeeze out as much liquid as possible from the spinach and chop finely. If using frozen leaf spinach, cook according to the instructions. Drain, squeeze out the liquid, and chop. Set aside.

Step Three Heat the oil or ghee in a heavy 30cm (12in), preferably non-stick frying pan over a medium–high flame. When very hot, add the mustard seeds. As soon as the seeds begin to pop (this takes just a few seconds), add the onion and garlic. Turn the heat to medium and fry for 3–4 minutes. The onions should turn very lightly brown at the edges. Now add the chopped spinach and keep stirring and frying for another 10 minutes. Add the cooked potatoes, 1 teaspoon salt, the garam masala and the cayenne pepper. Stir and mix gently until the potatoes are heated through.

Pumpkin Cooked in the Delhi Style

This is a family recipe. It was cooked chiefly on holy days and certain types of fasting days. We ate it with Poori (see page 191), a yoghurt dish, a potato dish and some pickles and chutneys. In India we would use a green pumpkin – probably, technically speaking, a gourd. The local name for it is *kashiphal,* or 'the fruit of the holy city of Benares'. I find that an ordinary pumpkin or any hard-skinned winter squash works just as well, and I usually make this with either pumpkin or hubbard squash. From a 1.5kg (3lb) segment, with skin, I am usually left with about 900g (2lb) of flesh.

Serves 4–6

Step One Put the oil or ghee in a large, wide, preferably non-stick pan and set over medium–high heat. When very hot, add the cumin seeds. About 10 seconds later, add the nigella, fennel seeds, fenugreek seeds, peppercorns and whole red chillies. Stir once or twice quickly, then add the pumpkin. Stir for 1 minute. Cover, turn the heat to low and cook for 40–45 minutes or until the pumpkin is just tender, stirring now and then and replacing the cover each time.

Step Two Uncover and add the salt, sugar and amchoor or lemon juice. Stir gently, mashing the pumpkin lightly so that you retain some texture. Serve hot.

Note

The whole chillies and peppercorns should not be eaten.

4 tablespoons vegetable oil or ghee

½ teaspoon cumin seeds

¼ teaspoon nigella seeds (kalonji)

¼ teaspoon fennel seeds

large pinch of fenugreek seeds

½ teaspoon black peppercorns

2–3 dried, very hot red chillies (of the cayenne type)

about 900g (2lb) pumpkin flesh, cut into 2.5–4cm (1–1½ in) cubes

¼–1 teaspoon salt

1½ tablespoons light soft brown sugar

2 teaspoons ground amchoor or lemon juice

V

143

Spinach with Paneer (Saag Paneer)

Saag paneer, a combination of greens and paneer, is eaten all over north India with slight variations in the spices. In India, the spinach, which turns into a sauce for the paneer, is sometimes creamed. At other times, it is left in its chopped state, thus allowing it to stand in equal partnership with the paneer. I like the latter method because this way the spinach retains its texture. For this recipe, I have used fresh spinach because I prefer its taste. You could use two packets of frozen, chopped spinach, though, if you like. Cook spinach according to packet directions, drain well, and proceed with the recipe. Do not salt the spinach twice and remember to cook it very briefly with the ginger–garlic mixture.

Serves 4–6

2.5cm (1in) cube fresh ginger, peeled and coarsely chopped

3–6 garlic cloves, peeled

½–1 fresh hot green chilli, sliced roughly

6 tablespoons vegetable oil

150–200g (5–7oz) paneer

salt

¼ teaspoon garam masala

¼ teaspoon cayenne pepper (optional)

675g (1½ lb) spinach, washed, trimmed, and very finely chopped

3 tablespoons single cream

Step One Put the ginger, garlic and green chilli into the container of an electric blender or food processor along with 50ml (2fl oz) water. Blend until you have a smooth paste. You may need to push down with a rubber spatula once.

Step Two Heat the oil in a large, wide, preferably non-stick sauté pan over a medium heat. Put in all the pieces of paneer and fry them, turning them over gently with a slotted spatula, until they are golden brown on all sides. (This happens fairly quickly.) Remove the paneer with a slotted spoon and place on a plate in a single layer. Sprinkle the paneer quickly with ⅛ teaspoon salt, the garam masala and the cayenne pepper. Set aside.

Step Three Put the paste from the blender into the hot oil in your pan (keep your face averted) and fry it, stirring constantly, for about 30 seconds. Now add the spinach and ½ teaspoon salt. Stir the spinach around for 1 minute. Cover the pan, lower the heat, and let the spinach cook gently with the ginger–garlic paste for 15 minutes. There should be enough water clinging to the spinach leaves to cook them. If all the water evaporates, add 1–2 tablespoons and continue cooking. Now add the paneer and cream, stir gently and bring to a simmer. Cover and continue cooking on low heat for another 10 minutes. Stir once or twice during this period.

Spinach with Ginger and Green Chillies

Indians tend to eat a lot of greens, sometimes a single variety by itself, sometimes mixed with other leaves. The most commonly available of all greens in the West is spinach and that is what I have used here. I keep the leaves whole, but if they are very large you might need to chop them coarsely.

Step One Cut the ginger, crossways, into very thick slices. Stacking a few slices at a time together, cut them into very fine slivers.

Step Two Put the oil in a wok or large, wide pan and set over high heat. When very hot, add the ginger. Stir until the ginger starts to brown. Add the spinach and chillies. Stir and cook until the spinach has wilted completely. Add the remaining ingredients. Stir and cook for another 5 minutes.

Serves 4

2cm (1in) piece fresh ginger, peeled

3 tablespoons vegetable oil

500g (1lb 2oz) trimmed, washed spinach

2–3 fresh hot green chillies, finely chopped

about ½ teaspoon salt

½ teaspoon store-bought garam masala

¼ teaspoon sugar

¼ teaspoon chilli powder

For more recipes from My Kitchen Table, sign up for our newsletter at www.mykitchentable.co.uk/newsletter

Vegetable Pullao

This recipe uses the Indian version of very slightly sprouted mung beans that are so nutritious and easy to digest.

Serves 6

185g (6½oz) whole mung beans, picked over and washed

long grain rice, measured to the 450ml (15fl oz) level in a measuring jug

4½ tablespoons vegetable oil

1 teaspoon whole black mustard seeds

1 medium onion, peeled and finely chopped

4 medium garlic cloves, peeled and finely chopped

1 teaspoon peeled, finely chopped fresh ginger

150g (5oz) string beans, trimmed and cut into 0.5cm (¼in) long pieces

100g (4oz) medium-sized mushrooms, diced into 0.5cm (¼in) pieces

2 teaspoons garam masala

1½ teaspoons ground coriander

2½ teaspoons salt

2 tablespoons finely chopped fresh green coriander, or parsley

Step One Put the mung beans in a bowl with 700ml (1¼ pints) water. Cover lightly and set aside for 12 hours. Drain the beans and wrap them in a very damp tea towel. Put the wrapped bundle in a bowl. Put this bowl in a dark place (such as an unused oven) for 24 hours.

Step Two Wash the rice well and soak in 900ml (1½ pints) water for half an hour. Drain well. Preheat oven to 160°C/325°F/gas mark 3.

Step Three Heat the oil in a wide, heavy, 5–5½ litre (8–10 pint) ovenproof pot over a medium–high flame. When hot, add the mustard seeds. As soon as the mustard seeds begin to pop (this takes just a few seconds), add the onion. Stir and fry for about 5 minutes or until the onion turns brown at the edges. Add the garlic and ginger. Fry, stirring, for about 1 minute. Turn the heat to medium–low and add the mung beans, rice, string beans, mushrooms, garam masala, ground coriander and salt. Stir and sauté for about 10 minutes or until the rice turns translucent and the vegetables are well coated with oil. Add 900 ml (1½ pints) hot water and the chopped coriander. Turn the heat to a medium–high flame and cook, stirring, for about 5 minutes or until most of the water is absorbed. (There will be 2.5cm (1in) or so of water at the bottom.) Cover the pot first with aluminium foil, crimping and sealing the edges, and then with its own lid. Place in the preheated oven for half an hour. Fluff up with a fork and serve.

Easy Chickpea Curry

I often make this spicy, north India-style curry, as it cooks easily and quickly. I use tinned chickpeas and, although it looks like a long list of seasonings, they actually all grind together in one go in the blender.

Step One Leave the chickpeas to drain in a colander.

Step Two Chop the tomatoes, ginger, garlic, chillies and coriander leaves and put in a blender with the ground coriander, cumin, turmeric, cayenne pepper, 1 teaspoon salt and 5–6 tablespoons water. Blend until smooth, pushing down with a rubber spatula when necessary.

Step Three Cut the potatoes into 2cm (¾in) dice. Finely chop the onions. Pour 3 tablespoons oil into a wide, medium, lidded pan and set over a medium-high heat. When the oil is hot, add the cinnamon, cardamom and bay leaves. Ten seconds later, add the onions and potatoes. Stir and fry for about 6 minutes or until the onions are lightly browned. Add the paste from the blender. Stir for a minute. Cover, reduce the heat to medium-low, and cook for 6–7 minutes, lifting the lid now and then to stir. Add the chickpeas, ¼ teaspoon salt and 250ml (8fl oz) water. Stir and bring to a simmer. Cover, and cook gently on a low heat for 20 minutes, stirring occasionally.

Serves 4–6

350g (12oz) drained-weight tinned chickpeas (from a 540g can)

2 tomatoes, about 225g (8oz)

5cm (2in) piece fresh ginger, peeled

4 garlic cloves, peeled

3–6 fresh hot green chillies

25g (1oz) fresh coriander leaves

1 tablespoon ground coriander

2 teaspoons ground cumin

½ teaspoon ground turmeric

½ teaspoon cayenne pepper

salt

2 medium potatoes, about 255g (8oz), peeled

140g (5oz) onions,

corn, peanut or olive oil

1 medium stick cinnamon

5 whole cardamom pods

2 bay leaves

Chickpeas Cooked in Tea

This is the trick that all the vendors at truck stops use to give their chickpeas a dark appearance. The tea – leftover tea may be used here – leaves no after-taste, it just alters the colour of the chickpeas. For speed, I have used tinned chickpeas and tomatoes. If you wish to substitute fresh tomatoes, chop them very finely and use 8 tablespoons instead of 4. This dish may be served with pitta bread, a yoghurt relish and some pickles or salad. It could also be part of a more elaborate meal with meat or chicken, a green vegetable and rice.

Serves 4–5

2 x 500g (1lb 2oz) tins chickpeas

175g (6oz) onions

3 garlic cloves

1–2 fresh hot green chillies

3–4 tablespoons green coriander

vegetable oil generous pinch of ground asafoetida

1 teaspoon cumin seeds

4 tablespoons tinned chopped tomatoes

2 teaspoons peeled, finely grated ginger

300ml (10fl oz) prepared tea (use a plain one – water may be substituted)

1 teaspoon salt

2 teaspoons ground roasted cumin seeds (see Tip, opposite)

1 teaspoon shop-bought garam masala

Step One Drain the chickpeas. Rinse them gently with fresh water. Drain again.

Step Two Peel and finely chop the onions and garlic. Slice the chillies into fine rounds. Coarsely chop the coriander. Put 4 tablespoons oil in a wide pan and set over medium-high heat. When hot, add the asafoetida. Let it sizzle for a second. Now put in the cumin seeds and let them sizzle for about 15 seconds. Add the onions. Stir and fry until the onions turn quite brown at the edges. Add the garlic and let it turn golden, stirring as this happens. Now add the tomatoes. Stir and cook them until they turn dark and thick. Add the ginger and give a few good stirs. Now add the chickpeas and all the remaining ingredients. Bring to a simmer. Turn the heat to low and simmer, uncovered, for about 10 minutes, stirring gently now and then. Taste for balance of flavours and make necessary adjustments.

Tip

To make ground roasted cumin seeds, put 4–5 tablespoons of the whole seeds into a small cast-iron frying pan and set over a medium heat. Stir the seeds and roast over dry heat until they turn a few shades darker and emit a wonderful roasted aroma. Wait for them to cool slightly and then grind them in a clean coffee grinder. Store in a tightly closed jar.

Have you made this recipe? Tell us what you think at www.mykitchentable.co.uk/blog

Chickpea Flour Pancakes with Tomato and Onion (Tameta Kandana Poora)

A few of these flavourful pancakes served with a green salad make a wonderful light meal, especially in the summer when tomatoes are ripe and delicious.

Step One Sift the chickpea flour, salt and cayenne into a bowl. Very slowly add 300ml (10fl oz) water, stirring constantly. Stop when the batter is still paste-like to get rid of all lumps, then continue adding the rest of the water. Add the cumin seeds, the tomato and onion. Mix well. Set the batter aside for 30 minutes.

Step Two Put 1 teaspoon oil in a 14–15cm (5½–6in) non-stick frying pan and set over medium-high heat. When hot, stir the batter from the bottom and pour about 4 tablespoons into the frying pan. Tilt the frying pan around to spread out the batter. Now drizzle another teaspoon of oil over the top. Cook the pancake for about 2 minutes, or until the base has golden-red spots. Turn the pancake over and cook the second side for a minute or until it too has golden-red spots. Remove the pancake to a plate and cover with an upturned plate. Make all the pancakes this way.

Makes 9–10 pancakes

225g (8oz) chickpea (gram or besan) flour

1 teaspoon salt

¼–½ teaspoon cayenne pepper

1 teaspoon cumin seeds

4 tablespoons peeled, seeded and finely diced tomato (about 1 medium tomato)

4 tablespoons finely chopped onion or finely sliced spring onions

about 7–8 tablespoons vegetable oil

Cold Chana Dal with Potatoes

In this dish the chana dal is first boiled and then mixed with diced, boiled potatoes, salt, pepper, cayenne pepper, roasted cumin and lemon juice. If you like, you can slice spring onions and add them as well. It is served at room temperature or, if you wish, just very slightly chilled.

Serves 4

75g (3oz) chana dal, cleaned and washed

1 teaspoon salt

3 slices peeled fresh ginger, about 2.5cm (1in) in diameter and 3mm (⅛ in) thick

4 new potatoes, boiled and diced into 1cm (½ in) cubes

⅛ teaspoon freshly ground pepper

1 teaspoon roasted, ground cumin seeds

2 tablespoons lemon juice, or 3 tablespoons tamarind paste

⅛–¼ teaspoon cayenne pepper (optional)

Step One Boil the dal in 700ml (1¼ pints) of water, with ½ teaspoon salt and the ginger slices. Cover and simmer gently for 1 hour. Drain. Discard the ginger slices.

Step Two In a serving bowl, combine the dal, ½ teaspoon salt and the remaining ingredients. Mix well. Serve with roast lamb or pork chops. Indians often eat this as a snack, at tea time.

North Indian Moong Dal

This is north India's most popular dal. It is eaten with equal relish by toothless toddlers, husky farmers and effete urban snobs! Dal is an excellent side dish to accompany most meat and chicken dishes. Pulses – dried beans, peas and lentils – are a staple in India and are eaten in some form or other on a daily basis in almost every Indian home. For those who are poor, they are often the only source of protein. While we talk of earning our 'bread and butter', Indians speak of earning their 'dal-roti' – roti meaning bread.

Step One Wash the dal thoroughly and place in a large heavy-based pan or cooking pot. Add 1.2 litres (2 pints) water and bring to the boil. Remove the froth and scum that collects on the surface.

Step Two Meanwhile, peel the garlic and ginger. Add the garlic, ginger, coriander, turmeric and cayenne pepper (if using) to the pan. Partially cover, lower the heat and simmer gently for about 1½ hours, stirring occasionally. When the dal is cooked, the consistency should be thicker than pea soup, but thinner than porridge. Add salt to taste and the lemon juice. Transfer to a serving dish.

Step Three Heat 3 tablespoons vegetable oil or ghee in a small cast-iron frying pan over a medium-high heat. When hot, add the asafoetida and cumin seeds and fry for a few seconds until the asafoetida sizzles and expands and the cumin seeds darken. Immediately pour the oil and spices over the dal and serve, with lemon or lime wedges and rice or bread.

Serves 6

275g (10oz) hulled and split mung beans (moong dal)

2 garlic cloves

2 slices fresh root ginger, 2.5cm (1in) square and 3mm (⅛ in) thick

1 teaspoon chopped fresh coriander leaves

1 tablespoon ground turmeric

¼–½ teaspoon cayenne pepper (optional)

salt

1½ tablespoons lemon juice

vegetable oil or ghee

pinch of ground asafoetida, or a tiny lump of asafoetida

1 teaspoon cumin seeds

to serve

lemon or lime wedges

Moong Dal with Browned Onion

Here, the rich taste of crisply browned onions flavours the beans. This tarka should, ideally, be done just before serving. Put the heated beans into a serving dish, prepare the tarka and pour it over the top so it floats on the surface. The crisp onion, browned red chillies and cumin seeds act as a garnish as well as a flavouring.

Serves 6

175g (6oz) hulled and split mung beans (moong dal)

¼ teaspoon ground turmeric

1–1¼ teaspoons salt

3 tablespoons vegetable oil, preferably corn or groundnut

½ teaspoon cumin seeds

generous pinch of ground asafoetida

3 dried red chillies (a medium-sized, cayenne type is ideal)

50g (2oz) onion, peeled and cut into the finest half-rings

Step One Pick over the mung beans, wash in several changes of water and drain. Put the split beans in a heavy-bottomed saucepan. Add 1 litre (1¾ pints) water and bring to the boil. Watch carefully so that the contents of the pan do not boil over. Remove the froth that rises to the top. Add the turmeric and stir once. Partly cover, turn the heat to low and cook very gently for 40–50 minutes, or until the beans are tender. Add the salt and stir to mix. Put the hot or reheated mung beans into a serving dish and leave in a warm spot.

Step Two Put the oil into a small frying pan and set the pan over medium-high heat. When hot, put in the cumin seeds. Let them sizzle for 10 seconds. Add the asafoetida and, a second later, the red chillies. Stir for 5 seconds or until the chillies darken. Now add the onion. Stir and fry for 2 minutes. Turn the heat to medium-low and cook, stirring, for another 2 minutes or until the onions turn brown and crisp. Pour the contents of the pan evenly over the surface of the beans. Serve immediately. (The whole red chillies add flavour and are decorative, but should be nibbled at only by those who know what they're in for.)

For a video masterclass how to chop an onion, go to www.mykitchentable.co.uk/videos/choppingonion

Yasmeen Murshed's Red Lentils with Five Spices

Most lentils and beans are boiled in the same way all over the world. It is the seasonings that make the difference. Here is the Bangladeshi version of red lentils, cooked with a final tarka of the five-spice mixture containing equal portions of whole cumin, fennel, mustard, fenugreek and nigella seeds. The spices may be mixed at home or bought ready-prepared as a mixture known by its Bengali name, panchphoran.

Step One Put the lentils, turmeric and half the sliced onion in a lidded pan with 1 litre (1¾ pints) water and bring to the boil. Do not let the pot boil over. Skim off the scum that rises to the surface with a slotted spoon. Partially cover with the lid, reduce the heat to low and cook for 40–50 minutes or until tender. Add the salt and mash the dal and onion well with a potato masher.

Step Two In a small pan, heat the oil until very hot. Add the red chillies. As soon as they darken, add the panchphoran. Stir once and add the remaining onion. Stir and fry until the onion turns reddish brown. Pour the oil and seasonings into the pan of lentils. Cover the pan quickly to trap the aromas.

Serves 4

175g (6oz) red lentils

¼ teaspoon ground turmeric

1 medium onion, sliced into very fine half-rings

1–1¼ teaspoons salt

2 tablespoons corn oil

1–2 whole dried hot red chillies

1 teaspoon panchphoran (see page 131)

Whole Green Lentils with Green Coriander and Mint

For speed, I use a pressure cooker although you could cook the lentils in an ordinary saucepan for 50–60 minutes. You would need to increase the water by 300ml (10fl oz). If you cannot get fresh mint, use more green coriander.

Serves 4

3 tablespoons vegetable oil

½ teaspoon cumin seeds

½ teaspoon black or yellow mustard seeds

pinch of ground asafoetida (optional)

1–3 dried, hot red chillies

100g (4oz) onions, peeled and cut into fine half-rings

2 garlic cloves, peeled and chopped

1 medium-sized tomato, chopped

175g (6oz) whole green lentils

¾ teaspoon salt

1 teaspoon ground coriander

½ teacup chopped green coriander

½ teacup chopped fresh mint

Step One Put the oil in a pressure cooker and set over highish heat. When hot, add the cumin and mustard seeds. As soon as the mustard seeds begin to pop – this takes just a few seconds – put in the asafoetida and the red chillies. Stir once. Add the onions, garlic and tomato. Stir for about 2 minutes or until the onions brown a bit. Now add the lentils, 800ml (1 pint 7fl oz) water, salt, ground coriander, green coriander and mint. Stir and bring to a simmer. Cover, turn the heat to high and bring up to pressure. Turn the heat down to low and cook at full pressure for 15 minutes. Take off the heat, reduce the pressure with cool water and serve.

Red Lentils 'Tarka'

Indians tend to eat protein-rich legumes with many everyday meats. Often, these are prepared with just a flavouring, or 'tarka', of whole cumin seeds, asafoetida and whole chillies popped in hot oil or ghee. Mustard seeds and a choice of garlic, curry leaves, onions, even tomatoes may be added to this tarka. I have used red lentils here, partly because they are sold by all health-food shops and make the shopping very easy, but mainly because they cook faster than most other traditional dals (split peas). Serve this dish with plain rice and a simple meat or vegetable. Yoghurt relishes and pickles make good accompaniments.

Step One Pick over the lentils and wash in several changes of water. Drain. Put in a heavy saucepan. Add 1.2 litres (2 pints) water and the turmeric, stir and bring to a simmer. (Do not let it boil over.) Cover in such a way as to leave the lid just very slightly ajar, turn the heat to low and simmer gently for 35–40 minutes or until tender. Stir a few times during the cooking. Add the salt and mix. Leave covered, on very low heat, as you do the next step.

Step Two Put the oil or ghee in a small frying pan and set over highish heat. When hot, add the asafoetida, then, a second later, the cumin seeds. Let the cumin seeds sizzle for a few seconds, then add the red chillies. As soon as they turn dark red (this takes just a few seconds), lift up the lid of the lentil pan and pour in the contents of the frying pan – oil as well as spices. Cover the saucepan immediately to trap the aromas.

Serves 6–8

350g (12oz) red lentils (masoor dal)

½ teaspoon ground turmeric

1¼–1½ teaspoons salt

3 tablespoons vegetable oil or ghee

generous pinch of ground asafoetida

1 teaspoon cumin seeds

3–5 dried hot red chillies

Red Lentils with Courgette (Vegetarian Dalcha)

The vegetable used in this dish is normally the bowling-pin-shaped, pale green bottle gourd, but here I have used the faster-cooking courgette. This is a speciality from the southern Indian city of Hyderabad. Rice and a yoghurt relish could be served on the side.

Serves 4

175g (6oz) red lentils (masoor dal), picked over

¼ teaspoon ground turmeric

salt

vegetable oil

4 cardamom pods

4cm (1½in) stick cinnamon

2 bay leaves

½ teaspoon cumin seeds

1 medium onion, peeled and very finely chopped

2 teaspoons peeled fresh ginger, grated to a pulp

3 garlic cloves, peeled and mashed

1 medium courgette, cut into 2.5cm (1in) rounds and then halved crossways

freshly ground black pepper

¼–½ teaspoon cayenne pepper

a few squeezes of lime juice

Step One Put the red lentils and 1 litre (1¾ pints) water in a heavy-bottomed saucepan and bring to the boil. (Watch carefully so that the contents of the pan do not boil over.) Remove the froth that rises to the top. Add the turmeric and stir once. Cover, leaving the lid very slightly ajar, turn the heat to low and cook very gently for 40–50 minutes, or until the lentils are tender. Add 1–1¼ teaspoons salt, just enough for the lentils, and stir to mix.

Step Two While the lentils are cooking, put 4 tablespoons oil in a non-stick frying pan and set over medium-high heat. When very hot, put in the cardamom pods, cinnamon, bay leaves and cumin seeds. Stir for a few seconds, then add the onion. Stir and fry until the onion pieces turn medium brown. Add the ginger and garlic. Continue to stir and fry for another minute. Now add the courgette, black pepper, cayenne pepper and ¼ teaspoon salt. Stir for 1 minute. Add 120ml (4fl oz) water. Cover, turn the heat to low and cook for 2 minutes.

Step Three Uncover, stir gently again and then empty the contents of the frying pan into the pan with the lentils. Stir gently to mix and cook on low heat for 1 minute. Squeeze lime juice over the top before serving.

Spicy Punjabi Red Kidney Bean Stew

If I am serving this for lunch, it is often the main dish, offered in old-fashioned soup plates with a dollop of thick, creamy natural yoghurt in the centre. Sometimes I sprinkle a little finely chopped fresh coriander or parsley over the yoghurt. I like to serve thick, crusty wholemeal bread on the side, but you can, if you prefer, eat the beans with rice or a bulghur pilaf. A salad and/or vegetable dish could also be served on the side.

Serves 4–6

275g (10oz) dried red kidney beans, picked over and soaked

2 teaspoons salt, or to taste

3 tablespoons vegetable oil

225g (8oz) finely chopped onions

1 tablespoon finely chopped garlic

1 tablespoon finely chopped fresh ginger

275g (10oz) peeled and chopped ripe tomatoes

2 teaspoons ground coriander

¼ teaspoon cayenne pepper

2 teaspoons ground cumin

1 fresh green chilli, finely chopped

1 tablespoon ground amchoor

Step One Drain the beans and put them in a saucepan with 1.5 litres (2½ pints) water. Bring to the boil. Turn the heat to low, cover and cook gently for 2–2½ hours, or until beans are very tender. Add the salt to the beans and stir to mix. Remove from the heat.

Step Two Put the oil in a wide, medium pan and set over medium-high heat. Add the onions. Stir and fry until the onions are a rich reddish-brown colour. Add the garlic and stir a few times. Add the ginger and stir once or twice, then add the tomatoes, coriander, cayenne pepper, cumin and green chilli. Stir and cook on medium heat for 5–6 minutes, or until the tomatoes are slightly reduced. Add the cooked beans and their liquid, together with the amchoor. Stir. Turn the heat to low and simmer gently for 10 minutes to marry all the flavourings. Serve hot.

Plain Basmati Rice

Serve this rice with almost any dish you like. I love it with Moong Dal, Lamb with Whole Spices and Onions, lime wedges and a cucumber relish of some kind.

Serves 6

350g (12oz) basmati rice

1¼ teaspoon salt

1 tablespoon butter

Step One Wash the rice well in cold water. Soak it in a bowl with 1.2 litres (2 pints) of water and ½ teaspoon salt for 30 minutes. Then drain.

Step Two Melt the butter in a heavy-bottomed pot over medium heat. Pour in the drained rice and stir for a minute. Add 500ml (18fl oz) water and ¼ teaspoon salt. Bring to the boil, cover, lower heat to very low, and cook for 20 minutes. Lift lid. Mix rice gently with fork. Cover again and cook for another 10 minutes, or until the rice is tender.

Basmati Rice with Spices and Saffron

Saffron not only imparts its enticing yellow–orange colour, but a delicious flavour to rice as well. I'll never forget my first introduction to saffron. I was in my early teens and on my first visit to Kashmir. We were riding through a valley and past a hill that was completely purple from all the crocuses growing there. I remarked on their beauty and was told by my Kashmiri companions that the flowers meant more than just beauty to them. One of the boys got off his horse, plucked a flower and brought it to me. He pulled the petals apart to reveal the orange stigma, which – on drying – becomes saffron. He told me that thousands of stigmas were needed to obtain a single tablespoon of saffron threads. No wonder this prized spice is expensive. Although this recipe calls for basmati, any long-grain, fine-quality rice can be used instead.

Step One Dry-roast the saffron in a cast-iron frying pan, cool slightly, then crumble into the warm milk and leave to soak for about 30 minutes.

Step Two Put the rice in a bowl and wash well in several changes of cold water. Fill the bowl with 1.2 litres (2 pints) fresh water, add ½ teaspoon salt and leave to soak for 30 minutes. Drain.

Step Three Heat the oil in a heavy-based pan or cooking pot over a medium heat. Put in the cardamom pods and cinnamon sticks and stir over the heat a few times. Add the rice and fry, stirring, for about 1 minute. Add 500ml (18fl oz) water and ¾ teaspoon salt. Bring to the boil, cover with a tight-fitting lid, reduce the heat to very low and cook for 20 minutes.

Step Four Gently, but quickly, fork through the rice to separate the grains and drizzle the saffron-infused milk over the rice to form streaks of colour. Re-cover and cook for a further 10 minutes or until the rice is done. Turn the rice onto a serving platter with a fork. Serve at once.

Serves 6

1 teaspoon saffron threads

2 tablespoons warm milk

350g (12oz) basmati or long-grain rice

salt

2 tablespoons vegetable oil

5 cardamom pods

2 x 7.5cm (3in) cinnamon sticks

Turmeric Rice

This yellow, lightly seasoned rice may be served with almost any Indian meal.

Serves 4–6

basmati rice measured to the 450ml (15fl oz) level in a measuring jug

3 tablespoons vegetable oil

3 cloves

1 bay leaf

4 cardamom pods

2.5cm (1in) cinnamon stick

2 garlic cloves, peeled and finely chopped

¼ teaspoon ground turmeric

1 teaspooon salt

2 tablespoons finely sliced chives or the green part of spring onions

Step One Put the rice in a bowl and wash well in several changes of water. Drain and leave in a strainer set over a bowl.

Step Two Put the oil in a heavy saucepan and set over medium-high heat. When hot, put in the cloves, bay leaf, cardamom pods and cinnamon. Stir once or twice and add the garlic. As soon as the garlic turns medium brown, add the rice, turmeric, salt and chives or spring onions. Stir gently for a minute. Now add 675ml (22fl oz) water and bring to a boil. Cover tightly, turn the heat down to very, very low and cook for 25 minutes.

Lemon Rice

In south India, this rice is flavoured with lime juice. At our New York restaurant, Dawat, we do a simpler version using both the juice and rind of lemons instead. This has proved to be very popular. Serve with Indian vegetable dishes, any bean dish, pappadums and a yoghurt relish, plus pickles of course. This is served at room temperature in south India, where it is generally quite balmy. In the colder West I like to serve this hot.

Step One Combine the rice, salt and 700ml (1¼ pints) of water in a medium saucepan and bring to the boil. Cover tightly, turn the heat to very low and cook for 25 minutes.

Step Two Put the oil into a large frying pan and set over medium-high heat. When hot, add the mustard seeds. As soon as the seeds begin to pop – a matter of seconds – put in the curry leaves. Stir once, then empty the contents of the frying pan over the rice. Add the lemon juice and rind. Mix gently with a fork or slotted spoon. Mix once again when turning into a serving dish.

Serves 6

475ml (16fl oz) measure basmati rice, washed and drained

1 teaspoon salt

2 tablespoons vegetable oil

1 teaspoon brown mustard seeds

15 fresh curry leaves (use fresh basil or holy basil leaves as an interesting substitute)

2–3 teaspoons fresh lemon juice

2 teaspoons finely grated lemon rind

Rice with Peas and Dill

This dish is just as good for the family as it is for dinner guests.

Serves 5–6

basmati rice measured to the 450ml (15fl oz) level in a measuring jug

3 tablespoons vegetable oil

3 cloves

4 cardamom pods

1 small onion, peeled and cut into fine half-rings

1 teaspoon salt

1 teaspoon store-bought garam masala

4 tablespoons finely chopped fresh dill or 1½ tablespoons dried dill

675ml (22fl oz) chicken stock (use water as a substitute)

1 teaspoon salt if using unsalted stock or water

150g (5oz) fresh or frozen peas, cooked for just 2 minutes in boiling water

Step One Put the rice in a bowl and wash well in several changes of water. Drain and leave in a strainer set over a bowl.

Step Two Put the oil in a heavy saucepan and set over medium-high heat. When hot, add the cloves and cardamom pods. Stir for a few seconds. Add the onion, stirring until it is brown. Add the rice, salt, garam masala and dill. Stir for a minute. Now add the stock and the salt, if needed, and bring to a boil. Cover very tightly, turn the heat to very, very low and leave to cook for 20 minutes.

Step Three Add the peas. Cook for another 5–7 minutes. Stir gently before serving.

Rice with Mushrooms and Mustard Seeds

Almost any variety of fresh, seasonal mushrooms may be used here. Ordinary white ones also work perfectly well.

Step One Put the rice in a bowl and wash well in several changes of water. Drain and leave in a strainer set over a bowl.

Step Two Put the oil in a heavy saucepan and set over medium-high heat. When hot, put in the cumin and mustard seeds. As soon as the mustard seeds begin to pop – this takes just a few seconds – add the onion. Stir and fry until the onion browns a little. Add the mushrooms and stir for a minute. Now put in the drained rice and stir for a minute. Add the stock and about ½ teaspoon salt if your stock is salted, 1 teaspoon salt if you are using water or unsalted stock. Bring to a boil. Cover tightly, turn the heat to very, very low and cook for 25 minutes.

Serves 4–5

long-grain rice measured to the 450ml (15fl oz) level in a measuring jug

3 tablespoons vegetable oil

½ teaspoon cumin seeds

½ teaspoon black or yellow mustard seeds

25g (1oz) onion, peeled and cut into fine half-rings

10 medium-sized mushrooms, sliced lengthways

675ml (22fl oz) chicken stock or water

salt

Rice with Black-eyed Peas

For Western meals, try serving this with pork or lamb roasts and chops. It is also good with roast duck. Or try it with a German or Polish sausage accompanied with grilled tomatoes and mustard or beetroot greens! For an Indian meal, have it with Pork in a Mustard Spice Mix (see page 99). Serve some kind of yoghurt dish with it.

Serves 6

100g (4oz) black-eyed peas (lobhia) soaked overnight in 600ml (1 pint) water with ½ teaspoon bicarbonate of soda

2 tablespoons vegetable oil

7 whole cloves

7 black peppercorns

350g (12oz) long-grain rice

1 teaspoon garam masala

1½ teaspoons salt

Step One Empty the black-eyed peas and liquid into a pot. Add 300ml (10fl oz) water and ½ teaspoon salt. Bring to the boil. Skim off all the froth. Cover and simmer gently for 4–5 minutes. Drain and discard the liquid.

Step Two In a 5-litre (8-pint) heavy-bottomed pot, heat the oil over medium heat. When hot, add the cloves and peppercorns and fry until they expand (10–20 seconds). Add the rice and black-eyed peas and fry for 5 minutes. Add the garam masala, 1 teaspoon salt and 700ml (1¼ pints) water. Bring to the boil, cover, lower the flame to very low, and leave for 30 minutes.

Step Three Lift the cover to see if the rice is done. If not, cover and cook for another 5 minutes. Turn off the heat. Covered rice will stay warm for 15–20 minutes. Place on a warm platter to serve, gently breaking lumps with the back of a large spoon.

Naan

Naan is a leavened flat bread shaped like a teardrop. It is best when cooked in the clay oven called the tandoor. While meats, chicken and fish grill on large skewers inside the tandoor, moistened naans are stuck to its walls to bake.

Step One Sift the flour into a bowl. Place the milk in a small pot and warm slightly. Remove from the heat. In another bowl, combine the egg, salt, sugar, baking powder, yeast, 2 tablespoons oil, yoghurt and 5 tablespoons of the warm milk. Mix well. Pour the mixture over the flour and rub it in with the hands. Add 1 tablespoon of warm milk at a time to the flour, and begin kneading. Add enough so that all the flour adheres and kneading is easy. You should have a soft dough. Knead well for about 10 minutes or until the dough is elastic. Form into a ball, brush with oil, cover with a damp cloth and leave in a warm place to rise. If the temperature is above 27°C (80°F) it should take only 2 hours, otherwise it may take about 3 hours.

Step Two Preheat the grill and brush 3 baking trays lightly with oil. Knead the dough again for a minute or two and divide into 6 balls. Flatten the balls one at a time, keeping the rest covered, and stretch them and pat them with your hands until you have a teardrop shape about 28cm (11in) long and 10cm (4in) wide. Do all the balls this way, placing 2 naans on each baking tray as you do so. Cover with moistened cloths and leave for 15 minutes in a warm place.

Step Three Remove the moistened cloths. Brush the centre portion of each naan with water, leaving a 1cm (½in) margin. Sprinkle the centre portion with the nigella or poppy seeds. Place the trays, one at a time, under the grill, about 6–7.5cm (2½–3in) away from the heat, and grill the naans for about 2½ minutes on each side or until lightly browned.

Serves 6

450g (1lb) plain white flour

about 200ml (7fl oz) milk

1 egg, beaten

¾ teaspoon salt

2 teaspoons sugar

1 teaspoon baking powder

½ packet dried yeast (1½ teaspoons)

2 tablespoons vegetable oil, plus a little more for brushing on dough later

4 tablespoons natural yoghurt

¼ teaspoon nigella seeds (kalonji), or poppy seeds as a substitute

Wholemeal Griddle Bread (Paratha)

These are flat, wholemeal breads, best made in a heavy, cast-iron frying pan or griddle.

Makes 6 big parathas

100g (4oz) wholemeal flour plus 100g (4oz) plain flour, or 225g (8oz) chapati flour

additional flour for dusting

½ teaspoon salt

about 9 tablespoons vegetable oil

Step One Put the flour and salt into a bowl. Drizzle 2 tablespoons of oil over the flour and rub it in with your fingertips. Slowly add about 175ml (6fl oz) plus 1 tablespoon water, gathering the dough together into a ball as you do so. You should end up with a soft dough. Knead the dough for 10 minutes and then make a ball. Put the ball in a bowl and cover the bowl with a damp cloth. Set the dough aside for half an hour.

Step Two Knead the dough again and divide it into six parts. Keep five parts covered with a damp cloth as you work with the sixth. Make a round patty out of it and then roll it out on a floured surface until you have a 15cm (6in) round. Dust with extra flour whenever necessary. Spread about 1½ teaspoons oil on the top of this round. Gather the edges of the round together, forming pleats as you go. Soon you will have a closed pouch. Give the top of the pleats a small twist to close the pouch. Dust the pouch lightly with flour and put it, pleated side down, on a floured surface. Roll it out until it is about 18cm (7in) in diameter.

Step Three Heat a cast-iron griddle or frying pan over a medium-low flame. When hot, spread a teaspoon of oil on it and slap the paratha onto its heated surface. Cook for about 2 minutes. The top of the paratha should now have turned fairly pale. Spread a teaspoon of oil over it with the back of a spoon. Cook for another minute or so, turning the heat down a bit if necessary. The first side should have developed some pale, reddish-brown spots. Turn the paratha over and cook the second side for about 3–3½ minutes or until it too develops pale, reddish-brown spots. Take the paratha off the fire and wrap in aluminium foil. Make all the parathas this way, stacking them in the same aluminium-foil bundle. Parathas may be reheated in the foil; place in the oven on 180°C/350°F/gas mark 4 for about 15 minutes.

Deep-fried Puffy Breads (Poori)

Pooris, for me, are the easiest of Indian breads and the first ones I teach in my cooking classes. These days, you can always buy ready-made naans, pitta breads and even chapatis from supermarkets or takeaways. But pooris you do have to make yourself. They are quite heavenly when freshly prepared. Chapati flour is sold by all Indian grocers. If you wish to measure the flour in volume, you will need to fill a measuring jug up to the 475ml (16fl oz) level.

Step One Put the flour in a bowl. Add the salt and mix it in. Drizzle the 2 tablespoons oil over the top and rub it into the flour with your fingers. Slowly add the milk or water to form a medium-soft ball of dough. Knead the dough for 10 minutes or until smooth. Form a smooth ball, rub it with a little oil and set it aside, covered, for 15–30 minutes.

Step Two Just before eating, put enough oil for deep-frying into a wok or deep frying pan and set over medium heat. As it heats, divide the ball of dough into 12 balls. Roll one ball out into a 13cm (5in) round. Keep it covered with cling film. Roll out all the pooris this way and keep them covered.

Step Three When the oil is very hot, lay one poori carefully over the surface of the oil without letting it fold up. It should sizzle immediately. Using the back of a slotted spoon, push the poori over and cook on the second side for a few seconds. Remove with a slotted spoon and keep on a large plate lined with kitchen paper. Make all the pooris this way and eat immediately.

Serves 3–4

225g (8oz) chapati flour or a mixture of 100g (4oz) sieved wholemeal flour and 100g (4oz) plain white flour

¼ teaspoon salt

2 tablespoons vegetable oil plus more for deep-frying

about 100–120ml (3½–4fl oz) milk or water

Indian Rice Flour Pancakes

Serve these spicy pancakes with a cup of tea for breakfast or as a snack. Chutneys, freshly made or the preserved kind, can be served on the side. These pancakes are almost like breads and may be eaten with a meal as well.

Makes 8 pancakes

150g (5oz) plain flour

120g (4½ oz) rice flour

1¼ teaspoons salt

250ml (8fl oz) natural yoghurt

2 teaspoons peeled and very finely chopped fresh ginger

2 teaspoons finely chopped fresh green chilli

2 tablespoons finely chopped fresh coriander

5–6 tablespoons vegetable oil

Step One Combine the plain and rice flours, salt and yoghurt in a food processor or blender. Add 175ml (6fl oz) water and process until you have a smooth batter. Pour into a bowl. Add the ginger, chilli and coriander. Stir to mix. (You can set this batter aside for several hours, refrigerating it if necessary.)

Step Two Put ½ teaspoon of oil in a non-stick frying pan and set over medium-low heat. When it is hot, remove about 5 tablespoons of the batter and drop it in the centre of the pan. Put the bottom of a rounded ladle or rounded soup spoon on the blob of batter and, using a continuous spiral motion, move it outwards in concentric circles. You should end up with an 18cm (7in) pancake. Drizzle another ½ teaspoon of oil over the pancake and 1 teaspoon just outside its edges. Cover and cook it for 4–5 minutes or until the pancake is reddish-brown on the base. Turn the pancake over and cook the second side, uncovered, for about 4 minutes or until it too has reddish spots. Put the pancake on a plate and cover with foil or an upturned plate. Make all the pancakes this way. You can reheat all the pancakes, well wrapped in foil, in a moderate oven for 15 minutes. You could also heat them, one at a time, in the microwave oven for 40–60 seconds.

Fresh Green Mango Chutney

You do need green mangoes for this recipe – really unripe ones in which the flesh has a greenish tinge and is quite sour. The recipe also requires that you soak ½ teaspoon fenugreek seeds overnight. If you do not have the time to do that, just put ½ teaspoon fenugreek seeds into the hot oil along with the cumin and other seeds. Stored in a closed jar in the refrigerator the chutney should keep for a couple of weeks – that's if you do not eat it up first. My recipe is for a mild chutney. If you want it hotter, increase the chilli powder. Mangoes vary in their sourness, so do taste the chutney a good 5 minutes before it is ready and then you can adjust the sugar and salt, if necessary.

Makes 600ml (1 pint)

Step One Soak ½ teaspoon fenugreek seeds in 6 tablespoons water overnight.

Step Two Peel the mango and cut the flesh off the stone. Cut into strips that are 5mm (¼in) thick and wide and 5–7.5cm (2–3in) long. If you are in a rush chop the flesh coarsely.

Step Three Set 4 tablespoons oil over a highish heat. When hot, put in ½ teaspoon cumin seeds, ½ teaspoon fennel seeds, ½ teaspoon mustard seeds and ¼ teaspoon nigella seeds. As soon as the mustard seeds begin to pop – this takes just a few seconds – put in the ginger. Stir and fry it for 2 minutes or until it just starts to change colour. Now put in the soaked fenugreek seeds with their soaking liquid as well as another 250ml water and ¼ teaspoon ground turmeric. Bring to a boil. Cover, lower the heat and simmer for 15 minutes. Add the mango, 1–1¼ teaspoons salt, 5–6 tablespoons sugar, green chillies and ½ teaspoon chilli powder. Stir to mix and bring to a simmer. Simmer, uncovered, on a medium-low heat for 25–30 minutes or until the chutney is thick and all the mango pieces are translucent and tender. Serve at room temperature.

fenugreek seeds

about 675–900g (1½–2lb) green, unripe mango or mangoes

mustard or olive oil

cumin seeds

fennel seeds

mustard seeds

nigella seeds (kalonji)

6cm (2½in) piece fresh ginger, peeled and cut into fine julienne strips

ground turmeric

salt

sugar

3–4 fresh hot green chillies

chilli powder

Fresh Red Chutney with Almonds

This is the chutney that is traditionally served with the 'Hamburger' Kebabs on page 107. I now like it so much I serve it with most of my meals. Instead of fresh hot red chillies, I have used a combination of red pepper and chilli powder. You may use the former, if you so wish. It will be much hotter. Also, walnuts may be used instead of almonds. Both would be traditional and authentic. This chutney may be kept in the refrigerator for a few days.

Serves 8

75g (3oz) red pepper (about half a de-seeded large one), coarsely chopped

20 large mint leaves or 30 smaller ones, coarsely chopped

2 tablespoons lemon juice

1 garlic clove, peeled and coarsely chopped

½ teaspoon chilli powder

½ teaspoon salt

freshly ground black pepper

1 tablespoon blanched, chopped or slivered almonds

1 teaspoon chopped dill (optional)

Step One Into the container of an electric blender, put the red pepper, mint leaves, lemon juice, garlic, chilli powder, salt and black pepper in the order listed. Blend until smooth. Add the almonds and blend again. A few bits of almond may be left unpulverised. Pour into a bowl and check for seasonings. You may now mix in the dill, if you wish.

Plain Tamarind Chutney
(Saadl Imli Ki Chutney)

This chutney is made to be eaten with grilled aubergines. It can be drizzled onto yoghurt relishes and soups, and onto salads of mixed fruit and vegetables. It can also, of course, be served as a relish.

Step One Put the tamarind concentrate in a small bowl. Slowly add 3 tablespoons hot water, stirring as you do so to make a paste. Add all the remaining ingedients and mix well.

Serves 6

2 tablespoons tamarind concentrate

¼–½ teaspoon salt

freshly ground black pepper

3 tablespoons sugar

¼ teaspoon cayenne pepper, or to taste

1¼ teaspoons ground, roasted cumin (see page 152)

Cucumber Raita

This familiar, refreshing, cool yoghurt and cucumber relish complements nearly all Indian meals. In the hot summer months, it really takes the place of a salad.

Serves 4–6

1 cucumber

425g (15oz) natural yoghurt

salt

freshly ground black pepper

½ teaspoon ground roasted cumin seeds (see page 152)

pinch of cayenne pepper (optional)

pinch of paprika

Step One Peel and coarsely grate the cucumber.

Step Two Turn the yoghurt into a serving bowl and beat with a fork until smooth. Add the cucumber, and season with salt and pepper to taste. Reserve a pinch of the roasted cumin for garnish; add the rest to the yoghurt with the cayenne. Stir to mix and check the seasoning. Cover and refrigerate until required. Sprinkle with the reserved roasted cumin and paprika to serve.

Yoghurt with Carrot and Sultanas

The taste of this takes me back to the hundreds of festive banquets I have attended where something of this sort – a sweet-and-sour relish – always accompanied the main meal. You may serve it in small, individual bowls, if you like. In that case, a teaspoon would be the best eating implement. It could also be served at the end of a family meal as a salad-cum-dessert.

Step One Put the yoghurt into a bowl. Beat lightly with a fork until smooth and creamy. Add the sugar, salt, chilli powder and carrot. Mix.

Step Two Put the oil in a very small frying pan and set over medium-high heat. When very hot, add the cumin and mustard seeds. A soon as the mustard seeds begin to pop – this just takes a few seconds – add the sultanas. Stir once and empty the contents of the frying pan – oil and all – over the bowl of yoghurt. Mix.

Serves 4

300ml (10 fl oz) natural yoghurt

½ teaspoon sugar

¼ teaspoon salt

¼ teaspoon chilli powder

1 medium-sized carrot, peeled and coarsely grated

1 tablespoon vegetable oil

¼ teaspoon cumin seeds

¼ teaspoon black or yellow mustard seeds

2 tablespoons sultanas

Tomato and Onion Relish (Timatar Aur Pyaz Ka Cachumbar India)

This relish can be eaten with almost all Indian meals.

Serves 4

2–3 medium tomatoes

1 medium onion

1 teaspoon roasted, ground cumin seeds

1 tablespoon lemon juice

salt

freshly ground black pepper

⅛–¼ teaspoon cayenne pepper

Step one Cut the tomatoes into 5mm (¼ in) cubes. Peel and finely chop the onion. Combine the tomato and onion in a serving bowl.

Step two Add the roasted cumin, lemon juice and salt, pepper and cayenne to taste. Toss to mix. Cover with cling film and refrigerate for 30 minutes.

10 9 8 7 6 5 4 3 2 1

Published in 2011 by Ebury Press, an imprint of Ebury
Publishing

A Random House Group company

Photography by Yuki Sugiura © Ebury Press 2011;
Photography pp18, 38, 46, 54, 84, 88, 122, 138, 146, 165,
167, 190 © Craig Robertson; Photography p25 © Gus
Filgate

Recipes © Madhur Jaffrey 2011

Book design © Woodlands Books Ltd 2011

All recipes contained in this book first appeared in *The
Essential Madhur Jaffrey* (1996); *Madhur Jaffrey's World
Vegetarian* (1998); *Madhur Jaffrey Step by Step Cookery*
(2000); *Madhur Jaffrey's Quick and Easy Indian Cookery*
(2001); *Madhur Jaffrey's Ultimate Curry Bible* (2003).

Madhur Jaffrey has asserted her right to be identified as
the author of this Work in accordance with the Copyright,
Designs and Patents Act 1988

The Random House Group Limited

Reg. No. 954009

Addresses for companies within the Random House
Group can be found at www.randomhouse.co.uk

A CIP catalogue record for this book is available from the
British Library

The Random House Group Limited supports The Forest
Stewardship Council (FSC), the leading international
forest certification organization. All our titles that are
printed on Greenpeace approved FSC certified paper
carry the FSC logo. Our paper procurement policy can
be found at www.rbooks.co.uk/environment

To buy books by your favourite authors and register for
offers visit www.rbooks.co.uk

Colour origination by Alta Image

Printed and bound in Great Britian by Butler, Tanner and
Dennis Ltd

Commissioning Editor: Muna Reyal

Designer: Lucy Stephens

Photographers: Yuki Sugiura, Craig Robertson and
Gus Filgate (see also credits above)

Food Stylist: SPK and Silvana Franco

Prop Stylist: Luis Peral

Production: Helen Everson

ISBN: 9780091940522